Unfinished Reconciliation
Justice, Racism &
Churches of Christ

Edited by Gary Holloway & John York

A·C·U
PRESS

Unfinished Reconciliation: Justice, Racism & Churches of Christ

A·C·U
PRESS

ACU Station, Box 29138
Abilene, TX   79699
www.acu.edu/acupress

Designed and composed by Nancy Love in Linotype Trajanus with
display lines in sanserif Lydian. Text faces designed by American,
Warren Chappell, between 1938-39 and issued in digital form in
1997.

Copyright © 2003

Gary Holloway & John York

Printed in the United States of America

ISBN 0-89112-073-4

Library of Congress Card Number 2003104122

To the memory of David Lipscomb (1831-1917),
in hopes that his spiritual children will follow his example
of trying to live the gospel through racial reconciliation.

Contents

The Authors

Lee Camp (Ph.D., Notre Dame University) is Assistant Professor of Bible at Lipscomb University.

Douglas A. Foster (Ph.D., Vanderbilt) is Associate Professor of Church History and Director of the Center for Restoration Studies at Abilene Christian University.

Kenneth Greene (D. Min., Fuller Theological Seminary) is Minister of the Metro Church of Christ in Dallas, Texas, and he serves as Chaplain for the Texas Army Reserves.

John Mark Hicks (Ph.D., Westminster Theological Seminary) is Professor of Theology at Lipscomb University, and he serves as Adult Education Minister at the Woodmont Hills Church of Christ in Nashville, TN.

Harold Shank (Ph.D., Marquette University) is Minister of the Highland Street Church of Christ in Memphis, TN, and he is the national spokesperson for Christian Child Care.

The Editors

Gary Holloway (Ph.D., Emory University) is Ijams Professor of Bible at Lipscomb University and Minister for the Natchez Trace Church of Christ in Nashville, TN.

John York (Ph.D., Emory University) is Associate Professor of Bible and Preaching at Lipscomb University, and he serves as one of the Preaching Ministers at Woodmont Hills Church of Christ in Nashville, TN.

Introduction

This book grew out of the Biblical Preaching Seminar at Lipscomb University, "Preaching Social Justice," in May 2001. Several preachers gathered to discuss how one moves from the text of Scripture to the sermon. Obviously, the biblical texts discussed centered on the justice, mercy, and reconciliation God desires.

God worked in an amazing way in that seminar. Through the power of his word, brothers black and white prayed together, wept together, and began to catch a vision of reconciliation.

You might find these essays from that seminar unsettling. At first, it may not seem so. The first eight chapters deal with biblical teaching on justice, compassion, and inclusion. There may be little there that offends. After all, no one who claims to follow a just and merciful God can be for injustice. Nevertheless, there are reminders in these studies that we have not always practiced what the Bible teaches concerning justice.

The reminders grow louder in chapters nine through thirteen, chapters that focus on the injustice of racism. The turn from injustice in general to racism in particular may seem unfair, but we are not claiming that racism, particularly between whites and blacks, is the only form of injustice in our society. However, racism is, especially for its victims, the most visible form of social injustice.

Many would disagree. Have we not made great strides in racial reconciliation? Aren't all of our churches integrated? Don't they at least have a handful of members from a minority race? Don't our schools forbid unequal treatment based on race? Don't they actively recruit minority students and teachers? Isn't this talk of racism overstated and even unfair to our spiritual ancestors and to good-hearted Christians?

It is true that one meets few overt racists in our churches. Nevertheless, racism remains as the consequence of maintaining the status quo in our churches, schools, economy, and country. Few would disagree with the biblical call for justice. But many times only those who are victims of racism actually see the injustice. Many well-meaning white Christians are unintentionally blind to both racism and other forms of social injustice in our society. Having never been denied equal treatment, they assume all receive it.

Racial injustice remains in our churches. We are still divided by race, not united in Christ; thus the need for strong language to shake us from our lethargy. If this book generates passion in our hearts, then perhaps passion can open our eyes to truth.

It is time for us in Churches of Christ to be shaken out of our ease in a society based on institutional racism. Instead, we must respond to the Chronicler's call to reconciliation. We must be captured by the prophetic vision of a God who longs for justice. Most of all, we must joyfully embrace the announcement from Jesus that the kingdom of God is where love of neighbor, not institutional self-interest, rules.

So we ask you, the reader, to come to this book with a pure heart and an open mind. Let the power of God's word lead you. If God's words bring you discomfort, anger, or even pain, he does it only to heal. His desire is for our reconciliation to him and to one another.

Minor Prophets

1   Justice From Above

Harold Shank

Preaching social justice from the Minor Prophets can raise numerous issues. Among the concerns raised are these three: (1) Do the Minor Prophets have anything relevant to say about justice and equity in today's society? (2) Is social justice an issue that concerns people in the pew? (3) Does preaching on social justice make a difference?

The following three chapters respond to those concerns in three ways: (1) The topic of social justice in the Minor Prophets will be approached *from above*, or from God's perspective. In a world confused about the nature of fairness and justice, the Minor Prophets speak of a God of justice who provides a definition of fairness and equity. (2) The Minor Prophets present social concerns from the viewpoint of the oppressed, *from below*. The Minor Prophets give voice to hurting people of long ago, reflecting the pain felt by people in today's pew. (3) The experiences of the Minor Prophets reveal that their preaching on social justice did make a difference. This section, *from the pulpit*, posits that today's preaching does make a similar difference in contemporary society.

This material does not offer a systematic approach to social justice in the Minor Prophets, but uses selected texts to speak to the three central concerns; other texts could be appropriately added. Nor does this essay seek to deal with all the Minor Prophets, but centers on limited material in Hosea, Amos, and Micah. Those who seek a more comprehensive analysis of social justice or the Minor Prophets might consult other sources.[1] The focus of this study is multi-faceted, seeking to persuade the minister to preach about social justice from the Minor Prophets, offering a perspective from which to begin, and providing material from which lessons might be constructed.

PREACHING SOCIAL JUSTICE FROM ABOVE

Much of what the Minor Prophets say concerns the difference between the plan God has for human society and the kind of world humans typically establish. Inequity, unfairness, injustice, and oppression often characterize that difference. These prophets approach this difference both from the perspective of God, whose dream for human society has been shattered, and the perspective of those in the human community who regularly experience pain and oppression. Since the human experience of injustice and oppression is highly subjective, it is helpful to establish some objectivity by identifying how the Minor Prophets define justice. Since the Minor Prophets speak on God's behalf, they convey to us a divine definition of what is just and fair in society.

This chapter will argue that the character of God leads him to act in certain ways toward his people. That character and those actions reveal a divine understanding of what it means to be just in human society. The material at hand is not an exhaustive or comprehensive treatment of the divine character. It does not chronicle the actions of God revealed in the Minor Prophets in any systematic way, but only uses a slice of the prophetic material to show how a prophet's reflection on God's nature and actions leads to an understanding of how God views and defines social justice.

THE CHARACTER OF GOD

Concern about unfairness in human relationships is rooted in who God is. The Minor Prophets contain numerous texts that describe his nature, including Hosea 1-3; Joel 2:13-14; Jonah 4:2; and Micah 7:18-20. Particularly, Hosea 2:19-20 offers a complexity of words that describe a God concerned about human relationships. These words appear in the extended allegory that begins the book of Hosea. God tells Hosea to marry an adulterous woman. The story tells of her unfaithfulness to Hosea, the birth and naming of their children, and Hosea's attempt to remarry her after she has left him. In the allegory, Hosea represents God, while Gomer, Hosea's unfaithful wife, symbolizes the unfaithful Israelites. At times in Hosea 1-3, the lines between Hosea's life with his wife and God's experience with Israel become blurred. The chapters alternate between images of pain and pleasure. Pain comes first, when God gives negative names to Hosea's and Gomer's children (1:2-9). Pleasure comes when those names are reversed (1:10-2:1). Pain recurs upon Gomer's unfaithfulness (2:2-13). In response, the text refers to former and future periods of pleasure (2:14-23). The attempt to win Gomer back brings pain (3:1-4). The prophet ends the allegory with a presentation of a more pleasant future (3:5). Hosea 2:19-20 appears in one of the pleasure sections where Hosea presents the dream of what might be. The betrothal image used here is intended to capture the human anticipation and excitement of a coming wedding and marriage to convey the expectation and hope God has for all divine-human interaction.

The NIV text of Hosea 2:19-20 mentions six qualities of God: "I will betroth you to me forever; I will betroth you in **righteousness** and **justice**, in **love** and **compassion**. I will betroth you in **faithfulness**, and you will **acknowledge** the Lord."

It is possible to read these six qualities in two ways. First, they might be understood as describing the character of the *relationship* that God seeks to develop with humanity. Instead of describing either the character of God or the qualities of humanity, these six words describe the *relationship* between God and humans. Second, these six words can also be understood to define the *nature* of God. These are the traits of character that God brings to the relationship and which empower the relationship. The NIV understands the text in the latter way. This presentation will follow that reading.

It would be a mistake to see these as separate qualities of God as if the divine being could be reduced to a set of propositions. This essay is not a demographic study of divinity, but it is an attempt to explain the nature of the God who seeks relationship with us. Although we must seek to understand the words individually, they cumulatively describe the being of God.

The first two words, "righteousness" and "justice," frequently appear together in the Old Testament, often as descriptions of God. Righteousness is a relationship word; justice is a legal term.[2] Righteousness arises out of God's desire to be in a genuine, kind, mutually beneficial relationship with humanity. It is a word that often describes God's being and his mission.[3] Justice calls for an adherence to an objective morality of right and wrong. The same Hebrew root is translated as "to judge." Justice is not simply an attribute of God, but his nature.[4] These two qualities of God work together. When humans fail to live with righteousness and justice, their failure affects God's very being. When an evil deed destroys a marriage, righteousness is breached in the severing of the relationship, and justice is violated in the breaking of a law. When one person abuses another, righteousness is defiled due to the damage done to the relationship; justice is ravished because a standard has been breached. Oppression of any kind is an offense to both the righteousness and justice of God.

The righteousness and justice of God are fueled by his love.[5] The Hebrew word cannot be translated by one English word.[6] It is this quality of God that propels him to seek human companionship. It is a deep love that will not quit, give up, or let go. It continues despite rejection, rebellion, and unfaithfulness.

Closely linked with God's love is his compassion.[7] It describes God's tender feelings for those who depend on him. The word for compassion comes from a root that means womb. Compassion is linked to the feelings a mother has for her unborn child or the concern one has for an orphaned child. When Hosea names his second child, he calls her "Not Loved," using the negation of this term.

God's intention toward humanity involves his faithfulness.[8] Linked to the Hebrew word for nurse,[9] God believes in people, seeks to nurture them, and remains faithful despite the lack of returned affection.

The divine goal for God's relationship with humanity is described by the word "acknowledge."[10] This Hebrew word has a range of meanings: sexual intimacy (Genesis 4:1), verbal acknowledgment (Hosea 6:3), intellectual understanding (Hosea 2:8), and exclusive devotion (Hosea 13:4). The NIV translation, "acknowledge," is too cognitive to capture all the Hebrew word intends. The English "know" or to "truly know" is what God seeks in Hosea. God desires to "know" people, and he also wants them to truly know him in return.

The character God brings to a relationship is the one he wants back from his people and the one he desires for all humans to have among themselves. Hosea sees that the overture God makes toward his people is not reciprocated. His love is not returned. His faithfulness to them is not matched by their faithfulness to him. His people are not treating each other with these qualities.

This divine desire is not original with the Minor Prophets, though. They do not initiate the biblical description of God. His character is expressed clearly in the law. God's love for all people (Deuteronomy 7:7-11) and his desire to be loved and respected by them (Deuteronomy 5:6-12; 6:4-5) depict a high standard for the way they are to treat each other (Deuteronomy 5:16-21), especially those most vulnerable (Deuteronomy 15:1-23). Such descriptions of the divine being appear regularly in the Psalms (Cf. Psalms 7:9-11; 9:8-9; 82).

Why God Sent the Minor Prophets

The Minor Prophets' affirmation of the character of God is not prompted by an alteration in God's character but by a change in Israelite society. Archaeological investigation reveals that from the thirteenth to the ninth centuries most Israelites enjoyed a similar standard of living, represented by a four-room house. In the eighth century, archaeology indicates a massive change in the nature of Israelite society with a wealthy and a poor section of the community.[11]

The biblical text also reflects this changing socio-economic background. Passages dating from early in the Israelite's national period suggest an economic and social equity among the people: Saul did his own plowing (1 Samuel 11:5); David brought a simple bag of groceries as a gift to the king (1 Samuel 17:17). The occasional abuse of the people by those in power caused great outrage (as in Ahab's abuse of Naboth, 1 Kings 21:1-29). With the coming of the eighth century (and the first three Minor Prophets—Hosea, Amos, and Micah), the situation changes: people in Hosea's hearing claim "I am very rich, I have become wealthy" (12:8); affluent women demand another drink (Amos 4:1); officials deprive the poor of their land (Micah 2:1-2); and slave labor becomes more common (2 Kings 20:20; 2 Chronicles 32:28-29; Jeremiah 22:13; Hosea 3:10). The inequity and abuse in the Israelite community were inconsistent with the nature of God and short of what God expected of his chosen people.

JUST ACTIONS

Despite the injustice and inequity that became a prevalent part of Israelite society, God, through the Minor Prophets, continued to seek a just, fair society and, more specifically, a community that reflected his character: a community that would condemn abuse and violence (Hosea 4:1-2; 6:8-11), critique those bringing about a "reign of terror" (Amos 6:1-14, especially verse 3), and dream of each person with his own fig tree and vine in a land of peace (Micah 4:3-4). Because of his nature—righteousness, justice, love, compassion, faithfulness, and desire for mutual acknowledgment—God acts. These actions are reflections of his character. The actions of God and his prophets communicate his concern for the relationship with his people and among his people. God is active, not passive, in seeking to restore social justice among his people, as seen in the following four examples.

1. *God visits Israel.* Micah 1:2-4 describes a theophany, an appearance of God on earth. According to Micah, his visit is not to say, "Good job," but it is destructive. God is displeased with the sins of both Israel and Judah. Those sins are not described in Micah 1, but in Micah 2-3 they are clearly defined as inequity and injustice. Micah's retelling of the theophany describes an angry God visiting his people to correct the injustices and inequity in society. Because the people have violated what he has envisioned for his community, he comes to correct and punish. Micah's poetic description of God's action makes a striking comment about God's intentions toward his people and his concern for equity and fairness.

Imagine the scene: the door of the heavenly temple flies open, bangs as it hits the door stop, and God comes down through the atmosphere. He lands on a mountain and it melts under his feet. He looks at the valleys and they crack open; things that never burned before melt like wax. He does all this in order to call his people to account for their sins. This theophany reveals that God is aware of human injustice, that he cannot be lulled to sleep by the manipulations of unjust people in the community, that he will only sit in heaven for so long before finally making a destructive visit to correct the wrongs. The angry God depicted in the theophany is upset because of the violations to his basic character. Plotting, manipulating, cheating, and treating others in unjust ways have replaced righteousness, justice, love, compassion, faithfulness, and mutual acknowledgment. God's actions both reflect and defend his character.

2. *God sends prophets.* God not only comes personally, but he also comes representatively through his prophets. God sends prophets to challenge the community, to convey his displeasure, and to remind them of his character and of his dreams for community. The prophets speak for God and call people to return to his standard. As his spokesmen, the prophets convey the nature of God. They challenge injustice and call for a change in "business as usual."

3. *God accuses his own people of injustice.* The people who are guilty of injustice are God's people. Micah 2:1-2 tells of people in ancient Jerusalem staying awake at night, thinking up ways to oppress others. The lights in houses were not people praying, but people plotting; not people reading the Torah, but people planning terror; not people getting home late from the Temple, but people returning home from oppressing the innocent. When morning came, they carried out their plans. The people in power are taking land and houses away from other people. According to Micah 2:9, "You [Israel] make victims of the children and leave them vulnerable to violence and vice."[12] The people practicing this injustice are God's people. These are not cruel Assyrians. These are not bloodthirsty Philistines. These are not the war-like nations of the ancient world. These are not people who sacrificed children on altars. These people being accused by God of injustice are those who read the Torah, go to Temple, pray for the Messiah, and preach about mercy, but treat each other with injustice (Micah 3:1-3).

Amos 1-2 makes the same point. Six abusive nations of

the world are condemned before the prophet critiques God's own people for abuse and inequity. Amos recalls how the Israelites themselves had once been in slavery, emphasizing that those once oppressed are not immune from oppressing others. Those who forget that God stands for the weak and abused are likely to injure the weak and take advantage of the innocent. Any form of oppression is an act of rebellion against God. Mistreatment of other people is a symptom of an unhealthy relationship with God. To avoid being the abusers and the unjust, Amos urges all people to stay close to God.

4. *God feels the pain of broken relationships.* Perhaps the most unexpected action of God in the Minor Prophets relative to justice is God's willingness to feel pain caused by broken relationships. Hosea 2:19-20, the same text that explores the nature of God, is part of a larger section of Hosea that describes the pain God feels when his relationship with his people is violated.[13] Hosea's point is that human unfaithfulness, whether horizontal—from one person to another—or vertical—from one person or an entire community to God—is painful. Hosea's allegory uses feelings that humans experience to express the way God feels. The text presents the feelings of aloneness, rejection, outrage, betrayal, humiliation, and deception. All these emotions show how God understands and experiences broken relationships.

Hosea's method is more like a love letter than systematic theology, more like a peek into God's diary than listening to one of the sermons in Amos, and more like an exploration through God's heart than a trip into his head. It is emotional, not cognitive. This is the story of a broken heart, not a dusty history book.

Compare what Hosea does regarding the nature of God

with the Gospels' presentation of Jesus. The Gospels tell what it is like when God becomes a man. They picture how God walks, talks, looks, and laughs. The Gospels put human flesh and clothes on God. Hosea moves in a different direction. He describes in human terms what it is like to *be* God, and he uses our emotions, concerns, and pains to describe what God experiences. The Gospels transport God from heaven to earth. Hosea transports us, in a sense, from earth to heaven. The Gospels are a door through which God walks to appear to us. Hosea is a window through which we can look and see the heart of God.

We cannot reduce Hosea 1-3 to a set of propositions. Hosea tells a story. God tells Hosea to marry an unfaithful woman named Gomer. Just as Hosea and Gomer must remain faithful to each other, so God and his people must remain faithful to each other. Just as Gomer becomes unfaithful to Hosea, so Israel becomes unfaithful to God. Gomer's unfaithfulness hurts the marriage and hurts the children. Israel's unfaithfulness hurts God. Through this allegory, Hosea provides a conduit into the heart of God. Just as Hosea and Gomer experience pain, this allegory tells us that God acts on behalf of his people by sensing their pain. Since the pains of Hosea and Gomer are human experiences, the prophet allows the listener to sense something of how God feels. The story asks us to wonder how we would feel in this situation. What if you came home from the office one day and found another person in bed with your spouse? What if you learned your mate had two children on the other side of town? Hosea experiences pain to better explain what God endures when humans disappoint him.

Hosea paints a portrait of pain in chapter 1 by giving his children strange names. The first child, "Jezreel," belongs to Hosea and Gomer. Jezreel is the name of a notorious battlefield, a place of death. It would be similar to naming a child "Auschwitz" or "Kosovo." The second child is called "Not Loved." This would be similar to calling a little girl "Ugly" or naming her "Dog." The third child's name was "Not my People." This name is equivalent to "Rejected" or "Go Away." When Hosea took his children to the market, people would say "There's Kosovo, there's Ugly, there's Rejected." Each time Hosea called them to supper, put them to sleep, sent them to school, and all the times he heard other children making fun of his kids, it tore at his heart. Hosea's allegory suggests that injustice does to God what calling a little girl Ugly for a week does to a parent. Many wonder how God could ask Hosea to do such a thing. But that is the point. God asks his prophet to experience intense personal pain to help us understand how God feels in the face of unfaithfulness and injustice.

CONCLUSION

Preaching social justice from the Minor Prophets might begin "from above" by investigating the character and actions of God as revealed through these spokesmen. God's concern for justice and equity arises out of his character and is evidenced in his actions. The portrait of God in the Minor Prophets is not a new one, since there is clear evidence of these qualities of God elsewhere in the Old Testament. Still, the inequity and abuse of eighth-century Israelite society prompted the first three Minor Prophets to raise these issues again in a significant and powerful way.

Looking at social justice "from above" grounds the definition of justice in the character of God. Other societal definitions of justice must be viewed in light of the nature and actions of God—especially in a time when, by God's own judgment, injustice and abuse have reached an alarming state. Those of us who preach cannot easily ignore the nature and actions of God relative to this issue, but we are called, like the Minor Prophets, to speak on behalf of God to a society that has failed to maintain God's relationship standards.

2   Justice From Below

Harold Shank

Human needs often dictate preaching topics. The minister may develop subject material for preaching by listening to members of the congregation or by giving ear to cultural trends. Additionally, the minister will be rooted sufficiently in Scripture to raise concerns informed by an understanding of the nature of God.

Many pulpits take up social justice on a regular basis. Others never raise the subject at all. This chapter calls for the minister to listen, not only to voices in the congregation and culture—which may be muffled—but also to give ear to the Minor Prophets as they amplify the sounds of the oppressed that often go unnoticed. *From below* means that preaching on social justice gives voice to the oppressed by listening to and speaking about what is happening among those who are most vulnerable, abused, and denied.

LISTENING TO OUR MEMBERS

The phrase, "That's not fair!" is a common response to life. The umpire makes a bad call. We say, "That's not fair!" The bully takes over on the playground. We respond, "That's not

29

fair!" The repair shop puts in a new alternator that breaks down after only two weeks, and then they will not refund our money. We agonize, "That's not fair!" When someone cannot get a job because of handicap, gender, or race, "That's not fair!" When a foster child's case is not heard in court, "That's not fair!" When a loved one dies in a drive-by shooting, "That's not fair!" We understand unfairness. Thinking about fairness or justice is probably more important to people in our pews than many realize. Most of us have been victims of injustice. On some level, all of us have even perpetrated injustice on others.

There are many indications that we, like the eighth-century Minor Prophets, also live in a time of injustice. Jonathan Kozol's *Amazing Grace* describes injustice done to children; he compares children who live in Mott Haven in the Bronx with children who live on the Upper East Side of New York City.[14] Ron Sider's *Rich Christians in an Age of Hunger* provides immediate access to a great deal of economic injustice in our society.[15] Spending an evening riding with an ambulance crew or a police officer will give additional evidence of injustice in our society. While the injustice that we endure is separated by nearly 3000 years from that of the Minor Prophets, we need to pay attention to the voices of ancient Israel.

LISTENING TO THE POOR OF THE EIGHTH CENTURY

Poverty. Oppression. The definitions of these two words form a foundation for preaching. Government defines poverty with reference to income and family size, but poverty changes in nature and definition depending on time, on place, and on which government or group is doing the defining. Poverty is also relative. The destitute in Third World countries are different from the destitute in the inner cities of the U.S. The poverty that A. S. Ward, E. H. Ijams, and A. M. Burton dealt with when they established the Central Church of Christ in Nashville in 1925 is different from the economic deprivation in the same homes and neighborhoods today.[16] Cultural definitions of poverty may change, but this material seeks a theological description of poverty.

One of the Minor Prophets to address this issue is Amos, who accuses North Israel of injustice. His was a different time. It was more agrarian. Communities were smaller. There were much stronger relational networks than many of us are used to experiencing. Amos describes the oppressors in different ways, yet the prophet nowhere condemns these people for their wealth, despite their oppressive ways.[17] Instead, Amos accuses them of injustice and describes their oppression through four specific words used to define the poor and six specific words used to picture the actions of the oppressors.[18] These ten words provide a useful context for providing a theological definition of injustice from below.

FOUR WORDS DESCRIBING THE OPPRESSED

The first word Amos uses is "righteous."[19] The word for righteous does double duty in Amos. First, it describes the character of God, the kind of relationship he wants to have with us, and the relationship he wants us to have with each other (see previous chapter). Additionally, Amos uses this word to portray the poor—the righteous. While some poverty is self-induced,[20] Amos is indicating, by using the word "righteous," that the oppressed people in mid-eighth century Israel did not cause their own poverty. Others in the community took away their land, cheated them in the marketplace, or defrauded

31

them in the courts. The oppressed people were innocent. Deuteronomy 15 raises this same issue.[21] Verse four says, "There shall be no poor among you." God dreamed that the Israelites would establish a community with no poor people, but Deuteronomy 15:7 states reality: "If there is a poor man among you. . . ." There will always be earthquakes, tornadoes, disasters, or famines by which innocent people become poor. Verse 11 adds, "There will always be poor people in the land" meaning there will always be an opportunity to perform the righteous, just, faithful action for those innocently poor.

The second word Amos uses to describe the oppressed is "needy."[22] It refers to someone lacking something. Needy people are in want, in need of help, and require deliverance. They lack power, water, food, clothing, or all of the above-and more. The word is also used to describe the fatherless, those who lack a parent. The poor have fewer choices in life than others. Some people in Northern Israel (Samaria) have summer and winter houses; others have no houses. Some have ivory beds; others have no beds. Some have imported food and beverages; others eat the sweepings off the floor. Some are secure in Mount Zion; others are subject to a reign of terror.

Poverty is also evidenced by the limited choices available to the poor. I have four pairs of shoes. Many poor people have only one pair of shoes. Some in our society eat out frequently and must decide which restaurant to go to, but for others, the choice is "do we have beans or corn?" Our house has nine rooms; many live in houses with two rooms. Poverty is often a matter of how many choices a person has.

The third word used by Amos is "poor," and it describes the relative nature of poverty.[23] The poor are the denied, the debtors, the slaves, those without protection or means of security. In sum, the poor are vulnerable. The wealthy can trample on them and oppress them because, by comparison, the poor lack protection. With no protection from the powerful, the poor are often victims.

Even in Amos' time, there is recognition of the changing nature of poverty. Poverty does not consist of falling below an absolute standard of income or housing, but rather reflects what one has in comparison to others. In Amos' time, those in need lived that way *because* others took their lands and goods in unjust ways.

Amos' fourth word is "oppressed."[24] This word expresses intense feeling or emotion while describing someone as meek, humble, or lowly. The RSV and the KJV often translate this word as "afflicted." Hence, it means to be broken-hearted, distressed, or in suffering. Poverty hurts. Poverty affects people physically, emotionally, and spiritually. Those who cannot provide for their families experience a loss of dignity and respect. Imagine, in the words of Amos, watching that wealthy woman trample on your mother (Amos 4:1). This word refers to the emotional response of the child-witness. Imagine knowing that a man and his son both had sexual relations with your sister (Amos 2:7). Imagine hearing your father has been trampled into the ground at the gate of the city (Amos 5:12). This word, "afflicted," describes the emotional response people experience during oppression.

Amos gives voice to the oppressed in ancient Israel, people who have become poor because of the actions of others, who have fewer choices than their more wealthy neighbors, who are unable to protect themselves, and who are pained and distressed by the circumstances of life. These four words join with six other words Amos uses to describe the oppressor and provide for us a theological perspective on injustice.

Oppressors are first described as those who "trample":[25] those who swallow up, devour, or snuff out. The word can also describe an animal in heat. Moreover, it has strong economic overtones and can refer to a greedy, selfish action. Tramplers are people who hurt others without regard for the lives they smash.

The second word is "oppress."[26] It means to defraud or wrong a person, and it is often used in Old Testament texts discussing war. To oppress is to harm others with violence, deceit, dishonesty, or overwhelming power. The oppressor has little interest in the feelings or the plight of those being hurt. It is the opposite of the righteousness, justice, love, and faithfulness that characterize God.

The third word is a different Hebrew word meaning "to oppress."[27] Here, "to oppress" means to bind up or to tie up and is used in the sense of besieging a city or barricading an area so no one can pass. Some versions translate it as "afflict." It is also used in the agricultural sense of binding up a crop harvested out in the field. As this word specifically relates to oppressors, its use signifies a restriction in the number of options a poor person has.

The fourth is another word for "trample."[28] It is used of a person treading on grapes. This word carries with it the connotation of a strong inanimate sense. The action of trampling on grapes, which have no feelings, is applied to what the oppressors are doing to the oppressed. They are insensitive. Those who are doing this trampling are unaware, do not want to be aware, are naive about, or are apathetic about what they are doing to others.

"Turn aside" is the fifth word.[29] It is used of pitching a tent or stretching out an arm. In Amos, the word has a legal sense. It implies movement—in this case, movement away from justice. When individuals come to court to receive justice, the oppressor turns them aside, denying them access. In Amos 2:7, the KJV says "turn aside the way of the afflicted," while the NIV has "deny justice." The word "deny" is this word. The NIV of Amos 2:8 has, "they lie down beside every altar on garments taken in pledge." The word for "lie down" is this same word. The KJV of Amos 5:12 says, "Turn aside the needy in the gate," while the NIV says, "Deprive the poor of justice in their courts." "Deprive" is this same word. The oppressors block another person's way to justice.

The sixth word is "to crush."[30] It means to break, describing physical damage done to the poor. The effect on the poor is similar to the results of the trampling expressed in two of the other words. Oppressors do physical harm either directly or indirectly by their actions.

These six words describe the nature of oppression witnessed by Amos in the mid-eighth century B.C. The words suggest that oppression involves economic, judicial, and physical repercussions. Just as the nature of poverty is multi-faceted, so its causes vary in methodology.

IMPLICATIONS OF THESE EIGHTH-CENTURY VOICES FOR CURRENT PREACHING

Understanding the state of those being treated unjustly in eighth-century B.C. Israel and hearing of the unfair actions being taken against them by the wealthy and powerful provide a view of social injustice from below. This view is communicated from the perspective of those actually experiencing the situations deemed so unfair and unjust by God that prophets were sent to speak to the injustices. Injustice, poverty, and abuse will differ from one time and place to another, but the voices that Amos amplifies provide a theological perspective from which to view the injustices of our own day. The state of the oppressed in ancient Israel raises several concerns that are pivotal for current preaching. At least four issues arise.

1. *The invisibility of one's own injustice.* Most people have said, at some point in their life, "It's not fair!" Most people have some taste of being subjected to injustice. However, the situation in the eighth century B.C. suggests that injustice is often invisible to the people perpetrating it. God sends Hosea, Amos, and Micah because the oppressors are unaware of what they are doing. They are so caught up in their own lives, maintaining their own lifestyle and standard of living, that they are not aware of their oppressive actions. These people have the music of their lives turned up so high that the cries of the poor are drowned out. The money ringing in the cash register makes such a commotion that the pleas of the poor are not heard. Fortunately, God hears the cries of the abused. God hears the cries even when we, who may be guilty of oppressive actions, do not.

2. *The impossibility of neutrality.* Many who experience the sense of "it's not fair" will take action to right the injustice done to themselves, but deny responsibility for correcting injustice to others for which they are not directly responsible. Amos had done no injustice to the people in Samaria, but he is not able to remain neutral about their abuse. Not only does he come to speak for those who have no voice, but he also demands that those who seek to remain neutral join forces

with him. Amos presents at least four positions concerning injustice: (1) those who are being treated unjustly; (2) those who are perpetrating the injustice; (3) those who are neither being treated unjustly nor doing the injustice, but who remain silent; and, (4) those who express solidarity with the oppressed. Amos, as a prophet of God, addresses the entire population of Samaria. It is because of the silence of the third group that the second group abuses the first (Amos 5: 12-13). There can be no neutral Switzerland in the realm of theological injustice. The God who will not remain neutral sends a prophet who cannot remain impartial to move his people from their uninvolved, uninterested neutrality into the fourth position, expressing solidarity with the oppressed by speaking and acting on their behalf.

3. *The inclusion of all society.* Amos addresses the entire society about injustice done to a segment of the community. He speaks to the whole nation (2:6), fathers and their sons (2: 7), the fast and the strong (2:14), soldiers (2:15-16), wealthy women (4:1), the courts (5:10), businesses (5:11), the nice parts of town (5:11), agribusinesses (5:11), religion (5:21-24), people in the arts (6:5), government and politicians (7:11), store owners (8:5), and food producers (8:6). In speaking to all segments of society, Amos maintains that when injustice flourishes, it concerns all people in a culture. The way in which a society treats its weakest members reflects on the character of the whole society (cf. Deuteronomy 15).

4. *The response to injustice is godliness.* Some respond to injustice with a call for riot or revolution. Political coups, protest marches, and acts of terrorism against those in power are common responses to injustice. Amos, instead, points

to godliness. Amos 5 states the case against Israel's social injustice. This chapter repeatedly calls Israel to "seek God." Chapter four links Israel's injustice to a lack of relationship with God: "Yet you have not returned to me." If people focus on God and the entirety of his Word, they will see injustice and act on it. If people are close to God, they will be less inclined to treat others with injustice. Treating injustice without turning people to God is like painting over rotten wood. The purpose of preaching on social justice is to bring people to know the righteous and just God.

CONCLUSION

Amos hears the cries of the oppressed in ancient Israel. Micah and Hosea also hear the pleas of those who are most vulnerable to the unjust actions of the wealthy and powerful. The Minor Prophets provide a model for ministers of all ages as those who not only hear the voice *from above*, but also listen for the cries *from below*. A dominant image of the Old Testament is that of the God who hears the cries of his people in Egypt. God's sending of the Minor Prophets is a continuation of that theme; those who listen to the cries from below become imitators of this very quality of God himself.

3   Justice From the Pulpit

Harold Shank

In the face of extensive sin and unfairness, those who preach often feel a sense of helplessness. Evil seems too great and injustice too deeply entrenched to oppose with simple preaching. Even after listening to the word *from above* on how fairness and equity arise out of the character of God, even after hearing the cries *from below*—the oppressed, both in the time of the eighth century and in the current day—many ministers lack the courage or confidence to raise these issues in preaching. Can preaching make a difference in an evil and unjust society? How can the minister raise the effectiveness of preaching about social injustice? This chapter begins by offering an insight into the effectiveness of one preacher and then concludes by identifying traits of these Minor Prophets that current ministers can emulate while preaching on social justice.

Did the Minor Prophets Make a Difference?

Hezekiah was a dominant force for justice and equity in the eighth century. He ruled from 715-686 B.C. 2 Kings 18 summarizes Hezekiah's righteous and just reforms. This

39

chapter will treat the material in two stages: Hezekiah's early life and Hezekiah's royal reforms. The opening two verses provide the background to King Hezekiah:

> In the third year of Hoshea son of Elah king of Israel, Hezekiah son of Ahaz king of Judah began to reign. He was twenty-five years old when he became king, and he reigned in Jerusalem twenty-nine years. His mother's name was Abijah daughter of Zechariah. (2 Kings 18:1-2)

Hezekiah has just graduated from the equivalent of King's University or Monarchy School. He is twenty-five years old and the most powerful man in the Israelite community. Before looking at the next twenty-nine years, the period we best remember from the life of Hezekiah, it is helpful to reflect on the previous twenty-five.

His parents were Ahaz and Abijah. Some texts call her Abi, perhaps a nickname. His father became king in Jerusalem when Hezekiah was nine. Ahaz seemed to have one rule about life: "Do what's best for Ahaz." Ahaz would worship any god in any temple if he thought it gave him some advantage. In 2 Chronicles 28:23, Ahaz says "I will sacrifice to them that they may help me." He knew what he was doing. He was doing what was best for Ahaz.

God was so unhappy with Ahaz that he sent him the prophet Isaiah (cf. Isaiah 7). Isaiah met Ahaz in the lower part of Jerusalem and presented the king with a message directly from God. Through Isaiah, God told Ahaz what to do, but Ahaz would not do it. The reason he would not was that he was doing what was best for Ahaz.

Hezekiah had several brothers. We do not know much about them, but one morning Ahaz and Abi came into the boys' bedroom, grabbed the brothers, dragged them to the valley, and burned them alive. Ahaz was doing what was best for Ahaz (2 Chronicles 28:3).

That is the home environment in which Hezekiah grew up. According to the opening chapters of Isaiah, it was a time of injustice and paganism. Raised by a selfish, egotistical father, it would be reasonable to suspect that Hezekiah lived in fear of being the next son sacrificed in the valley.

Recorded in 2 Kings 18:3-8, the royal reforms instituted by Hezekiah define the second part of his life:

> He [Hezekiah] did what was right in the eyes of the Lord, just as his father David had done. He removed the high places, smashed the sacred stones and cut down the Asherah poles. He broke into pieces the bronze snake Moses had made, for up to that time the Israelites had been burning incense to it. Hezekiah trusted in the Lord, the God of Israel. There was no one like him among all the kings of Judah, either before him or after him. He held fast to the Lord and did not cease to follow him; he kept the commands the Lord had given to Moses. And the Lord was with him; he was successful in whatever he undertook. He rebelled against the king of Assyria and did not serve him. From watchtower to fortified city, he defeated the Philistines, as far as Gaza and its territory.

Hezekiah became a reformer. He changed the face of Jerusalem. He ended child sacrifice in the Kidron Valley. He ended pagan worship. By doing the exact opposite of his father—by obeying God—Hezekiah became known as a righteous and a just king.

Why?

Hezekiah is raised in paganism in a city filled with injustice. He is raised by a selfish, egotistical father who does only what is best for himself. He lives in fear that he will be the next sacrifice in the valley, but he grows up to become a man of God. Why?

Rolland Wolfe, in his commentary on the book of Micah in *The Interpreter's Bible*, says that the reason is recorded in Micah 1:8, one of three autobiographical verses in Micah. "For this I will lament and wail. I will go stripped and naked. I will make lamentation like the jackals and mourning like the ostriches." Micah preached in Jerusalem, walked street-to-street, square-to-square, wailing, crying, preaching, and warning. "This wailing campaign of Micah may have been an important factor in causing King Hezekiah to make the sweeping reformation in the early part of his reign."[31]

Micah was a country boy who moved to the city and who preached barefoot and naked. People said his sermons sounded like the wails of a jackal, an ostrich, or an owl. He appeared on the scene for just a moment, a blip in Israelite history, but it is likely that he changed the life of a young man named Hezekiah. The influence of Micah the preacher on the man who would be king was more powerful than that of Hezekiah's own mother or father. Once Hezekiah was influenced, the whole nation was changed.

It is a striking insight into how God works. Just when it seems things cannot get any worse, God sends someone to stand in the gap. He sends a preacher, someone such as Micah, who influences a young king-to-be, changing a nation.

Beyond the difference that Micah made in the life of Hezekiah, these Minor Prophets have had a towering influence over all subsequent history. Of all the books of the ancient world, why have these small works been preserved? Through the call to justice in these Minor Prophets, many have been influenced for righteousness and justice. What made their words so effective? What elements of their lives and preaching can produce the same results in current preaching?

QUALITIES OF THE MINOR PROPHETS THAT ENDURE

The three Minor Prophets who spoke out about social justice in the eighth century do not reveal a great deal about themselves. Yet, when we view these prophets through what they preached about social justice, four timeless qualities are revealed.

1. *The Minor Prophets knew their times.* In addition to archeological discoveries, Hosea, whose writing demonstrates familiarity with the Baal culture, is a critical source for information pertaining to Baal theology. Amos witnessed worship at Bethel and Gilgal and saw oppression in the city. He knew women were being abused and raped. He had seen people trampled into the ground. He understood the culture. Additionally, Micah knew what was going on in rooms where evil was being plotted (Micah 2:1). He cried out against the oppression and sin he saw (Micah 1:8).

All of this suggests that preachers must know something of their culture. A couple of years ago, several of us hired Ray Bakke, one of the foremost experts in America on urban ministry, to give us an informational tour of urban ministry in Chicago. Bakke, a white man with a doctorate, lives and raised his family in the inner city of downtown Chicago. Our day with Bakke in Chicago was a life-changing experience for me because he understood Chicago. He knew where Mrs. O'Leary's cow had kicked over the lantern. He showed us Mrs. Daly's home and the unmarked Chicago police car sitting in front of her house; one like it has been there for forty-five years. On another street he said, "All the houses were built by the Polish when they moved here. The two-by-fours start at the basement and go all the way to the attic. When they catch fire, the house burns in minutes." He took us to two restaurants, side by side. A man who was related to the Shah of Iran owned one, and someone who had lived on the same street as Saddam Hussein operated the other. He knew why the African Americans on one side of Chicago did not vote for Harold Washington and why the African Americans on the other side pushed him into office.

I was embarrassed. I did not know my city like he knew his. When I returned home, we got all of our church staff on a bus and toured Memphis. We saw the corner where our predecessors had lynched a black man. We went into the basement of a house where slaves had been kept and saw the tracks of the railroad that led down to the river. We went to the spot where a black man who could not swim rescued 100 white people, including my neighbor, from a sinking ship.

To be like the Minor Prophets, who had a clear-eyed knowledge of the places where they lived, we would do well to know what God and Satan have been doing in the places where we live.

2. *The Minor Prophets were personally involved in ministry.* Hosea was told to go and marry. He went and married. It is not a parable; it happened. Hosea's wife committed adultery and then left. He became a single parent. Hosea 11 was probably written about twelve to fifteen years after chapters 1 through 3. Hosea, with three children, two of them not even his, faced being a single parent to teenagers. Looking at it through those eyes, we get a sense of this man's personal involvement in his ministry.

Amos left home, got a visa, and crossed through Passport

Control into another land. In this new land, the king's personal priest opposed Amos, who watched the powerful trample the vulnerable into the ground.

Then there is Micah. Nine times Micah calls the suffering people in Jerusalem "my people." He hurt along with their hurting. He felt the heavy foot of injustice trampling on him. Micah even faced opposition from other prophets (Micah 3). These three Minor Prophets were personally involved with the people to whom they were ministering.

Involvement in ministry validates the message about justice. Every minister can find some way to experience things that will validate the message: riding in an ambulance, working at a homeless shelter, serving at a work camp, sitting in the courthouse and talking to people waiting for trial, or visiting with the people in the unemployment line. Visit the childcare people in your community and cry with them as they talk about how the courts refuse to hear the cases of foster children.

People follow their leaders, children imitate parents, and students emulate their teachers. Likewise, churches echo their preachers. The minister's personal involvement in justice and injustice has a powerful influence within both the congregation and the community.

3. *These Minor Prophets knew the power of a dream.* Hosea married Gomer, a woman of prostitution, and saw in her a faithful wife. Amos could look at a land that had almost no rivers and see justice flow like a river, view righteousness as an ever-flowing stream. Micah imagined huge crowds of people from all directions, marching to Zion. He could see every person with his own fig tree and her own vine.

Hosea, Amos, and Micah went against the flow. Their

dreams were not what the common people of that time had in mind for their future. These Minor Prophets were not swayed by the cultural majority. Through God, they saw a different kind of world that God would create. There is power in a vision.[32]

Somebody in every community must see people flowing to Zion to hear the word of God. Someone must see a vision of the nation hammering military hardware into plowshares and spears into pruning hooks. Someone must paint a picture of a society where each person has his or her own fig and vine. Dreamers do not have dreams; dreams have dreamers. The dreams come from God, not from us.

Unfortunately, many people do not like dreamers. That is one reason why they did not like the prophets. Dreams mean change: the end of sinful ways, comfortable lives, and inward-focused churches. People and preachers tend to forget dreams. The prophets were dreamers, and they knew the power of a vision to accomplish what could never be done otherwise.

These Minor Prophets kept these dreams alive by preaching. Hosea, Amos, and Micah were preachers; their sermons survived. Their message changed a nation. Their words continue to challenge the world today. The most powerful weapon against indifference and injustice is the preaching of the word of God; the word of God continues to transform culture.

4. *The Minor Prophets were filled with passion.* Hosea's words throb with energy, emotion, and enthusiasm. Amos begins his book by recording what God had done through him: "God thundered and roared." A key autobiographical text of Micah is 3:8: "But as for me, I am filled with power, with the spirit of the Lord, and with justice and might to declare to Jacob his

transgression, to Israel his sin." The Minor Prophets were men of energy, enthusiasm, and passion.

Imitating these Minor Prophets calls today's minister to preach with passion, to take the offensive. The world does not change by maintaining the status quo. It changes by aggressive, dominant, marching ahead, risk-filled preaching. We learn from Amos 7 that those who preach about social justice will get complaints. Amos heard the complaints, but kept on preaching.

CONCLUSION

These Minor Prophets who spoke about injustice were knowledgeable about their culture, personally involved in social justice, aware of the power of presenting a vision through preaching, and passionate about their work. Perhaps all of these factors played a role in Micah's influence on Hezekiah, influence that transformed an entire nation. What is most clear, though, is that God called his prophets to speak about social justice. They did, and their message made a difference both then and now.

Chronicles

4 Justice & the Heart of God

John Mark Hicks

Chronicles may seem like a strange place to reflect on a biblical ethic of social justice. Chronicles, for example, is not the most well-read section of the biblical canon. Indeed, for many years Chronicles was the stepchild of Old Testament scholarship. It has always taken second chair to 1-2 Samuel and 1-2 Kings. Moreover, some regard Chronicles as theologically vacuous and irrelevant. For example, McKenzie wrote, "It is difficult to imagine any theological question asked in this generation on which the book of Chronicles is likely to shed any light."[33]

However, the Chronicler is a narrative theologian. He writes theological history. While a historian in that he makes factual claims about the past, he is a theologian who uses history to proclaim a theological message. At the heart of the Chronicler's message is the faithfulness of a God who seeks a people for himself, a people after his own heart who also seek him.

The Chronicler bridges the gap between his generation and the canon of the Old Testament available to him. He had the Pentateuch, Samuel-Kings, some of the prophets, and some of the Psalms in front of him (as well as non-canonical sources). He attempted to make sense of God's work in Israel in his postexilic situation. As an interpreter of Scripture, he applied the meaning of God's promises to his own context. As a narrative theologian, he retold the history of Israel through the eyes of God's dynastic promise to David and his redemptive promise to Solomon through the temple. He restored hope to his discouraged postexilic community.[34]

The Chronicler's story is the story of God's search for a people who seek him. This story means that God seeks to shape a people into his own image and to impart to them his own values. The heart of God yearns to commune with a people who yearn to commune with him. At the core of that heart is a concern for mercy and justice within community, and this is the principle concern of contemporary discussions of social justice.

THE SETTING AND FUNCTION OF CHRONICLES

Chronicles covers the same historical period as Samuel-Kings. Consequently, we have two histories of Israel, much as we have four histories of Jesus (Matthew, Mark, Luke, and John).

While the two histories cover the same period, they write in different settings, with different purposes, and for different audiences. 1-2 Kings was compiled during the Babylonian exile. Exilic questions were "Why were we exiled?" or "Do the Babylonian gods overrule Yahweh?" or "Where are God and his promises?" 1-2 Kings focuses on the sins of Israel and Judah. David and Solomon do not escape judgment, and the whole nation is judged for its sins. Judah is in exile because it sinned, which is also to assert that in actuality, the Babylonian gods did not win, but rather Yahweh, who controls Judah's destiny, removed Judah from their homeland. 1-2 Kings explains God's judgment against both Judah and Israel.

Chronicles was written during the postexilic period, that is, after the return of the exiles from Babylon in 536 B.C. The Chronicler's audience lived in Judah and their postexilic questions differed from the earlier exilic ones. The postexilic community asked "Will God still dwell among his people in his temple?" or "Will God take us back as his people?" or "Will God keep his promise to David?" While the Chronicler explains the exile as a divine judgment, he stresses God's yearning to restore his people. God will keep his promises, and God will dwell among his people as in the days of Solomon. If the postexilic community will seek God, then he will dwell among them. 1-2 Chronicles articulates God's gracious attitude toward all Israel, including both Ephraim and Judah.

The primary significance for the Chronicler's first readers was the assurance that the Davidic covenant was still operative and that God dwelled among his people in his temple just as he did in the days of Solomon. God yearns for his people, and he will keep his promises; God returns the exiles to the land in order to dwell among them. Indeed, the climax of Chronicles is the decree to rebuild the temple (2 Chronicles 36:22-23). Chronicles, therefore, offers the postexilic community a gracious hope.

For Christians, the story of God's graciousness culminates in Jesus Christ. The presence of God in the temple is the presence of the Holy Spirit in Christians. God seeks a people who seek him. God seeks worshippers (John 4:23-24) and yearns to share his communion with people who trust him with all their hearts. Just as the Exodus is our story, so the building of the temple is our story. When Christians study Chronicles, they study the significance of God's temple-building for their own faith and life. They learn something about God's faithfulness and grace; about worship, holiness, faith and perseverance; and about the God of David and Solomon, who is also the God of Jesus Christ.

THE THEOLOGY OF CHRONICLES

The fundamental theological hermeneutic of Chronicles is "God seeks seekers." The faithful and gracious God seeks hearts that seek him. The God of Chronicles is a relational God who seeks authentic, reciprocal relationship. Those who seek him will be found by him, but he will forsake those who forsake him (1 Chronicles 28:9; 2 Chronicles 15:2).

Two of the most significant terms in Chronicles are "seek" and "heart." They are thematic for Chronicles.[35] These terms are linked 11 times (1 Chronicles 16:10; 22:19; 28:9; 2 Chronicles 11:16; 12:14; 15:12,15; 19:3; 22:9; 30:19; 31:21), that is, hearts that seek God. "Seek" appears 54 times (the most in biblical literature) and "heart" 64 times (only Jeremiah and Psalms use it more often). God seeks hearts and yearns for hearts that seek him.

The flip side of God's relational nature is that he will forsake those who forsake him (1 Chronicles 28:9; 15:2). The history of Israel is filled with example after example of this God-forsakenness. Ultimately, because Israel forsakes God, God forsakes Israel.

Consequently, God enters history to create, discipline, probe, test, and redeem in order to find hearts that seek him as he seeks them. Chronicles is the story of Yahweh who moves among his people to know their hearts and find those who seek him (2 Chronicles 16:9). In Chronicles, Yahweh creates the world and preserves a people throughout history (1 Chronicles 1-9). Yahweh establishes a covenant with David as he inaugurates a kingdom (1 Chronicles 17). Yahweh graciously dwells among his people in the temple (2 Chronicles 6-7). Yahweh disciplines, blesses, and tests his people in order to know their hearts (1 Chronicles 29:17-19; 2 Chronicles 32: 31). The story of Chronicles is the dynamic engagement between God and his people as God seeks to establish a gracious relationship with those who seek him.

The Davidic promise involves God's commitment to rule the nations through Israel. The move from Sinaitic theocracy to Davidic kingdom was not incidental. The postexilic restoration was incomplete without a Davidic king, although the temple was fully operational. The Davidic promise grounds the hope of the restored community in a future Davidic king. The postexilic community depends on God's faithfulness to David.

However, the Davidic kingdom finds its pinnacle in God's presence in his temple. God comes to "rest" among his people (2 Chronicles 6:40-42) as they rest in the land God has given them through Davidic victories. The temple is God's redemptive, gracious, and reconciling presence. It is the place of communion between God and his people. The postexilic community must trust the gracious presence of God in the temple.

Thus, standing on the promises of God to David and the gracious presence of God in the temple, the postexilic community is called to hope, holiness, and perseverance. If they will seek God in his temple, trusting in his promises, then God will find them and give his gracious, reconciling presence to them.

THEMATIC TEXTS (1 CHRONICLES 28:9)

> And you, my son Solomon, acknowledge the God of your father, and serve him with wholehearted devotion and with a willing mind, for the Lord searches (literally, "seeks") every heart and understands every motive behind the thoughts. If you seek him, he will be found by you; but if you forsake him, he will reject you forever.

The general orientation toward God is described as seeking the Lord. "If you seek him, he will be found by you; but if you forsake him, he will reject you forever." The contrast between seeking and forsaking is strong. They are two modes of life. The seeker yearns for God and is devoted to him with a whole heart and a delighted soul (cf. 2 Chronicles 6:38). This expresses the integrity and basic direction of a person's life. A seeker finds peace and joy in serving God. The forsaker, however, yearns for something or someone else. The forsaker rejects God to serve other gods, the opposite of seeking God. Solomon is given this fundamental choice—the choice we all have—of seeking or forsaking God. It is the choice God gave humanity in Eden, and it is the choice that yet remains.

David, however, does not leave the "seeking" to Solomon alone, Chronicles shows. God "seeks" Solomon. God seeks ("searches") every heart. The nation's leaders and Solomon are to seek ("follow" in 1 Chronicles 28:8,9) and yearn for God. In the same way, God seeks and yearns for Solomon, that is, he seeks or yearns for every heart (cf. Isaiah 55:6). This is divine initiative and purpose. God seeks a people for himself, a nation where he can be their God and they will be his people. Thus, "Yahweh's 'seeking' would thus be understood as a kind of longing, rather than as the scrutiny suggested by" the NIV and NRSV.[36]

The noun in 1 Chronicles 4:23 represented by the

NIV's "every motive behind" describes the task of potters. Its use describes shaping or molding thoughts. The verb "understands" is causative, which means "to give understanding" or "to cause to understand" (cf. Psalm 119: 34, 73). God gives understanding. God is engaged with his world to shape them into his own image. He seeks to reorient hearts toward himself.

God desires a reciprocal relationship (cf. the verb "seek" in Psalm 119:2, 10, 176). Yahweh, a relational God who yearns and longs for his people, actively shapes a people for himself (e.g., gives understanding, cf. Psalm 119:27, 34, 73, 125, 130, 169). He keeps their heart and molds them as a potter does clay. This is how God approaches every heart. God continues seeking a people. He is active in the world as he seeks those who are seeking him (cf. Acts 17:27; Hebrews 11:6; John 4: 23). God's "'seeking out' of 'all hearts' is a search for response, not judgmental so much as longing."[37] McConville applies this insight to the history of God among his people:

This means that, by virtue of the creation-commitment, God's heart naturally goes out to man (seeking), and finds rest only when *he* finds rest. God's activity in v. 9 is therefore the seeking of a responsive heart…. The one who does not seek God is unworthy, in the strongest possible sense, of God's commitment to him, because he does not conform to God's own ancient and enduring decree concerning what constitutes true humanity…. It remains simply to notice that the idea of God's commitment to humanity in creation comes to its ultimate expression in the Incarnation. There is a sense in which the Incarnation is not a new intensity of commitment to humanity on God's part. The radical nature of that commitment was implied in the act of creation itself. It is because creation is *for relationship* that it brings in its train such possibilities, on the one hand, for *enjoying* God, and on the other—by the refusal to respond to him—for causing him offense.[38]

2 CHRONICLES 7:14-16

If my people, who are called by my name, will humble themselves and pray and seek my face and turn from their wicked ways, then will I hear from heaven and will forgive their sin and will heal their land. Now my eyes will be open and my ears attentive to the prayers offered in this place. I have chosen and consecrated this temple so that my Name may be there forever. My eyes and my heart will always be there.

Solomon's prayer has ended (2 Chronicles 6). 2 Chronicles 7:14-16 is a programmatic divine response for the Chronicler. It is the core of his theology and provides the principle that is worked out in the coming Divided Kingdom narrative (2 Chronicles 10-36).

2 Chronicles 7:14 is a well-known verse in Chronicles. It has been the thematic verse for revivals throughout history. Its significance for Chronicles is clear. It appears in a divine oracle and offers hope to fallen Israel. Whenever Israel finds itself in the midst of a drought, a crop devastation, or a plague, their hope is in God. Consequently, throughout the history of God's people, 2 Chronicles 7:14-16 has been recalled repeatedly to revive hope among broken people.

Its language is soaked in theological meaning. God's intent is openness. His disposition is inviting—"my eyes will be open and my ears attentive." The sacrifices and prayers of God's people are means of mercy, and the temple epitomizes God's graciousness. God seeks to provide forgiveness and healing. This is what God desires, and he comes to dwell in the temple, his sanctuary, as a testimony of his intent. God declares, "My eyes and my heart will always be there."

But God seeks seekers (cf. 1 Chronicles 28:9). He takes the initiative. He yearns for a reciprocal relationship with his people—he seeks them and they seek him. Consequently, God will act in the world in such a way as to turn the hearts of his people to himself. God will even afflict his people in order to engender authentic relationship with him. As the Psalmist writes, "in faithfulness you have afflicted me" (Psalm 119:75). God is faithful to his intent: he will find seekers, and he will use all available means (cf. 2 Chronicles 24:19) to turn his rebellious children into seekers.

The response God seeks is described in 2 Chronicles 7:14, and this coordinates with God's own response. If Israel will (1) "humble themselves," (2) "pray," (3) "seek my face," and (4) "turn from their wicked ways," then God will (1) "hear from heaven," (2) "forgive their sin," and (3) "heal their land." Given the principle that God seeks seekers, 2 Chronicles 7:14 summarizes the theology of Chronicles. It is a message for the postexilic community—God is willing to hear and forgive if his people are willing to seek him. It is the message for the people of God throughout history—God will hear those who seek him.

However, God seeks a responsive chord from his people. He seeks authentic relationship. Consequently, God's forgiveness and healing is conditioned on the hearts of his people. To emphasize this, Chronicles describes the people's approach with four significant terms.[39] "Humble" appears 19 times (only 17 times in the rest of the Hebrew Bible)—often in reference to the humility God demands in his presence (2 Chronicles 12:6-7, 12; 30:11; 32:26; 33:12, 19; 33:23; 34:27; 36:12) or to God's act of humbling his people (2 Chronicles 28:19). "Pray" occurs 15 times (including 1 Chronicles 17:25; 30:18; 32:20; 32:24; 33:13), but it occurs ten times in 2 Chronicles 6-7 alone (6:19, 20, 21, 24, 26, 32, 38; 7:1, 14). "Seek" has a theological sense eight times (1 Chronicles 16:10, 11;

2 Chronicles 7:14; 11:16; 15:6, 15; 20:4). Its Hebrew synonym (also translated "seek") is found in 1 Chronicles 16:11; 28:9; 2 Chronicles 12:14; 15:2, 12, 13; 30:19; 34:3, 21, 26. "Turn" is a synonym for repentance (2 Chronicles 6:24, 37, 38; 7:14; 15:4; 19:4; 30:6, 9; 36:13). This heaping of terms (the only time these four verbs occur together) probably represents some kind of progression. If they will humble themselves, pray to him, seek his face, and turn from their sin, then God will hear, forgive, and heal.

2 Chronicles 7:13-14 evidences God's desire for relationship and 2 Chronicles 7:12, 15-16 testify to God's gracious disposition. He yearns to show mercy, but he will only show mercy to those who humbly seek him. Chronicles receptively demonstrates this principle—Rehoboam (2 Chronicles 12: 12), Asa (2 Chronicles 15:1-15), the northern pilgrims (2 Chronicles 30:11, 18-20), Hezekiah (2 Chronicles 32:24-26), Manasseh (2 Chronicles 33:12), and Josiah (2 Chronicles 34:27).

God's relationship with his people is reciprocal. If they seek him, he will be found because he seeks them. If Solomon and subsequent kings remain faithful, God will bless their reign. But if they forsake him, he will forsake them, unveiling the relational nature of God and his desire for communion with a people who want communion with him. God seeks all hearts (1 Chronicles 28:9), but the issue is whether or not there are any who seek him. Nevertheless, God remains The Seeker. He will keep his promise to David by raising up an eternal king in the person of Jesus Christ.

This is the question that faces the postexilic community: are they God-seekers? Their current temple pales in comparison to Solomon's. They have no Davidic king on the throne. They see the insignificance of Jerusalem in the Persian Empire. Yet, they remember God's great reversal in the Babylonian exile. Their question is, "Will God remember his great love for David? If we seek God, will he be found?" Although their second temple cannot be compared with Solomon's, "Will God hear our prayer, forgive, and heal if we seek him?" The resounding answer of the Chronicler is "Yes" (cf. 2 Chronicles 6:36-39). God seeks seekers (cf. Hebrews 11:6).

2 CHRONICLES 33:12-13

In his distress he sought the favor of the Lord his God and humbled himself greatly before the God of his fathers. And when he prayed to him, the Lord was moved by his entreaty and listened to his plea; so he brought him back to Jerusalem and to his kingdom. Then Manasseh knew that the Lord is God.

This is not only the core of the Manasseh narrative, but it is also the theological heart of Chronicles itself. The exile, repentance, and restoration of Manasseh is the story of Judah. God's gracious acceptance of penitent Manasseh is God's gracious acceptance of penitent postexilic Judah. It is a witness of God's gracious acceptance of all seekers.

The language of 2 Chronicles 33:12-13 abounds with Solomon's dedication language in 2 Chronicles 6-7. Both passages envision a moment of distress (2 Chronicles 6:28; 33:12) and people who seek ("entreat" here but synonymous with "seeking") the face ("favor") of God ("before you" in 2 Chronicles 6:24; 33:12). Both envision humility (2 Chronicles 7:14; 33:13) and prayer (2 Chronicles 6:19, 20, 21, 24, 26, 32, 34, 38; 7:14; 33:13). In both, God listened (2 Chronicles 6:19-21, 23, 25, 27, 30, 33, 35, 39; 7:12, 14; 33:13). In both, the prayers are characterized as pleas (2 Chronicles 6:19, 29, 35, 39; 33:13), and God "returns" the seekers to their privileged status (2 Chronicles 6:25; 33:13; cf. 2 Chronicles 6:37-38). When God's people turn to him, he returns to them (cf. 2 Chronicles 7:14). Manasseh, as the Hebrew text emphatically notes with the addition of the pronoun "he," "knew that the Lord he is God." Thus, as in the prayer of Solomon, God makes himself known by his graciousness (2 Chronicles 6:33; 33:13).

In other words, Manasseh's humbling repentance and prayer is a specific instantiation of Solomon's temple prayer. God is faithful; he keeps his promises. If his people will seek him—wherever they are (Babylon or postexilic Judah)—God will graciously find them.

CONCLUSION

God gave his presence to the Solomonic temple as a place of forgiveness (sacrifice) and reconciliation. It was the place where the people of God could seek God's mercy. But he also gave his presence as a means of justice within the community. Solomon's temple is a place where the people of God could seek divine justice. God's "resting" place is a place of holiness and justice as well as mercy. To seek God means to share God's values in terms of both justice and mercy. God expects his people to seek his face but also to share his values as a community.

The temple is a place of justice because it is where God dwells. Solomon's prayer in 2 Chronicles 6 envisions six scenarios—the middle four call upon God to "hear and forgive" (2 Chronicles 6:24-33). The first and sixth, however, call for divine justice (2 Chronicles 6:22-23, 34-35). In particular, the first scenario (2 Chronicles 6:22-23) asks God to "judge" between the "guilty" and the "innocent" (righteous) who have been falsely accused. Innocent victims seek justice in God's temple courts. In other words, Solomon seeks the right of imprecation, that is, to give justice over to God. He seeks redress for the innocent who has been falsely accused (cf. Psalm 7).

The Chronicler is concerned about mercy and justice because the character of God is concerned about mercy and justice. David is a paradigmatic king because he did "what was just and right for all his people" (1 Chronicles 18:14). God gave Solomon the throne so he could "execute justice and righteousness" (2 Chronicles 9:9). If the people of God seek God, they must also seek mercy and justice. If the people of God do not seek mercy and justice, they do not seek God, and God will forsake them.

The relational root of social justice is the fact that God seeks seekers who share his values and his heart. God seeks hearts that are yearning to show mercy and do justice as he does (Micah 6:8), and hearts that understand that he desires mercy more than sacrifice (Hosea 6:6; Matthew 12: 7). Whether the people of God proclaim, seek, and work for social justice is an indication of whether or not they truly seek the God of Israel whose heart is filled with faithfulness, mercy, and justice (cf. Matthew 23:23).

5   Justice, Wealth & Power

John Mark Hicks

Social justice has two sides. On one side are the victims of injustice who experience oppression. On the other side are the wealthy and powerful who enable injustice, ignore injustice, or, worse still, pursue unjust means and goals. The God of Israel sympathizes with the victims and tests the wealthy and powerful.

Although the term "test" rarely appears in Chronicles, its theological import is pervasive.[40] This perspective must supplement the more common idea of "immediate retribution" which refers to God's immediate divine judgment upon sin in Chronicles. This often explains the wars, setbacks, and economic problems encountered by Judah. These events are divine retribution. However, not all such problems are the function of punishment. Some are divine testing.

The function of testing mitigates any hard rule of "reward and punishment." God is still sovereign and may use all available means to test hearts.[41] Immediate retribution, then, is not a mechanistic force in the cosmos (like "karma"), but a tool in the hands of a personal, sovereign God who sometimes tests wealthy and powerful, yet pious, kings.

This testing motif fills the story line of Scripture. Abraham is tested (Genesis 22:1). Israel is tested (Deuteronomy 8: 1-5). Job is tested (Job 23:1-12). Jesus is tested (Matthew 4: 1-11). Paul is tested (1 Thessalonians 2:4). Believers are tested (Judges 2:22; 3:4; Psalm 17:3; 66:10; Isaiah 48:10; Zechariah 13:9; 2 Corinthians 8:8; James 1:12). The world is tested (Revelation 3:10). Believers pray for testing (Psalm 26:2; 139: 23). Just as God seeks hearts, he tests them.

The story of Hezekiah provides a primary example of testing in Chronicles. 2 Chronicles 29-31 details Hezekiah's reform in the first months of his reign. But 2 Chronicles 32 summarizes three episodes (Assyrian invasion of Judah, Hezekiah's illness, and the visit of the Babylonian envoys) which occurred ca. 701 B.C. as divine testing. The issue is whether Hezekiah will continue his trust in the Lord throughout his reign or whether he will vacillate as did other kings who started out well but nevertheless ended badly (e.g., 2 Chronicles 25-27). These three episodes test Hezekiah's faith.

When Jerusalem is threatened, when his own life is at stake, when his political reputation is on the line, whom will Hezekiah trust? Pride is the issue. Through trials such as the three presented in 2 Chronicles 32, God probes the hearts of his people. Despite Hezekiah's wholehearted devotion to God in his reform (2 Chronicles 31:21), God tests Hezekiah to know what is in his heart (2 Chronicles 32:31; cf. Deuteronomy 8:2). The moment of testing unveils the heart (cf. Genesis 22:12).

Testing the Wealthy

In 1 Chronicles 28-29, David gathers Israel for a liturgical coronation of Solomon as king. David calls this gathering an "assembly of the Lord" (1 Chronicles 28:8) and invites those gathered to "praise" God (1 Chronicles 29:20; cf. 29:1, 10). David construes this praise as the responsibility to offer wealth to God by supporting the building of the Temple.

David reminds the leaders of Israel of God's gracious election of Israel and God's dynastic promise to David (1 Chronicles 28:2-7). He then charges Solomon and the leaders to seek God just as God seeks them (1 Chronicles 28: 8-10). David seeks to solidify support among the people in 1 Chronicles 29 for his temple plans. His purpose is to engender support for the new temple—both in terms of recognizing it as a divine work and sharing personal wealth for its construction. Just as Moses sought free-will offerings for the support of the tabernacle (Exodus 25, 35-36), so David seeks free-will offerings for the support of the temple. The people respond generously to David's plea for support.

THE RESPONSE (1 CHRONICLES 29:6-9)

Rather than commanding the people to set aside personal resources for the temple, David endeavors to persuade them. The beginning and end of the appeal are important. The beginning is communal; the task is great and Solomon needs help. Although Solomon is God's "chosen one," he is still "young and inexperienced." Even God's elect servants need community. The community must help build God's "palatial structure."

The final appeal, though, is inspirational in character: "Now, who is willing to consecrate himself today to the Lord?" The verb "consecrate" literally means "to fill the hand," which is technically "associated with the induction of a priest into his office" (cf. Exodus 28:41; 29:29; 32:29).[42] The dedication of gifts to the Lord is a priestly act on the part of Israel. The act of sacrificial giving is also a priestly act; it is a sacrifice to the Lord (cf. Hebrews 13:16). Thus, "it is not simply the gift that is consecrated to God but the giver. As one bids the gift farewell, one takes on a new role before God, a role of consecration to the service of God."[43]

The leaders of Israel responded generously. The term "gave willingly" is used seven times in 1 Chronicles 29 (5, 6, 9[2], 14, 17[2]; cf. Exodus 25:21, 29). The people saw the gifts of their leaders and "rejoiced" just as David did (1 Chronicles 29:9). Rooted in the spiritual significance and generosity of the gifts, the joy expressed the leaders' wholehearted devotion "to the Lord" (1 Chronicles 28:9; 29:9). This was not about a building per se. Rather, it was an act of priestly dedication fitting for a holy nation that God intended to be a "kingdom of priests" (Exodus 19:5).

DAVID BLESSES THE LORD (1 CHRONICLES 29:10-20)

This is one of the most paradigmatic prayers in Scripture. Steeped in theological significance for both David and the Chronicler, the prayer acknowledges that the kingdom belongs to God as well as the whole earth. It thanks God for the grace he has demonstrated to Israel and his dynamic activity in the world for the sake of his people. It appeals to God's heart to move in the hearts of Israel. The prayer assumes a dynamic, active God who yearns for his people and supplies their every need. This confidence evokes praise, but it also evokes a confidence that enables generosity. Paul makes a similar appeal to the Corinthians in a didactic context (1 Corinthians 9:6-15). David does it in a liturgical prayer (God is addressed seven times directly). Even though this prayer speaks to God, it also teaches God's people.

David's prayer is a blessing ("praised" is literally "blessed" in 1 Chronicles 29:10). The blessing links the present experience of Israel to the past and secures the future. The eternal God is the Lord who was with "Israel" (Jacob), and who is now with David. The assurance that David draws from the eternal God as the God of his "father Israel" also assures the postexilic community.

This blessing (1 Chronicles 29:11-12) reflects Israel's worship language. The doxological language of greatness, power, glory, and splendor ascribes to God what rightly belongs to him as the sovereign Creator. He fills the earth and all majesty belongs to him. While the Lord reigns over all the earth and everything belongs to him, on this occasion God has demonstrated his reign in Israel. The references to "wealth and honor" refer to the occasion of dedicatory gifts to the temple and to the enthronement of Solomon. Thus, the reign of God over Israel is manifested in the election of Solomon and the wealth that flows to the temple. In his sovereignty, God has gifted Israel with wealth.

The heart of the prayer is David's reflection on Israel's situation before this sovereign God (1 Chronicles 29:13-17). It acknowledges that God is actively testing Israel with this gift of wealth. God's gifts to Israel enable their gifts to him.

The praise of 1 Chronicles 29:13-17 contrasts the greatness of God and the frailty of humanity. The first part emphasizes human dependence (1 Chronicles 29:13-16), while the second stresses human integrity (1 Chronicles 29:17). Thanksgiving comes from the recognition that "everything comes" from God's "hand" (1 Chronicles 29:14, 16). With the realization that God has given this wealth for the building of the temple comes the concomitant praise and thanksgiving. The generosity of the people depends upon the generosity of

God. Generosity does not flow from pride, but from humility. It flows from dependency, not self-sufficiency.

This humility and dependency are metaphorically expressed in 1 Chronicles 29:15. Just as "father Israel" in 1 Chronicles 29:10 recalled Israel's patriarchal heritage, so also the language of "aliens and strangers" recalls her itinerant beginnings (Genesis 23:4; also 17:8; 21:23). This was the plight of Israel's forefathers, and Israel continued its pilgrimage, David says. This seems a bit out of place, however, now that Israel has territorial integrity. How can Israel still be an alien and a stranger? Israel sojourns among the nations as God's people. It is a spiritual pilgrimage "in your sight," that is, literally, "before your face." Israel has always had a sojourner status before God, confirmed by this allusion to the brevity of life.

While 1 Chronicles 29:14-16 stresses human dependency and divine graciousness, 1 Chronicles 29:17 stresses human integrity. Integrity is a proper response to divine testing. God is engaged with humanity through testing or probing their integrity—as demonstrated in Job (Job 1-2; 23:10). God actively seeks a people for himself through testing. God is pleased when his people reciprocate.

David recognizes this occasion as a test, and he rejoices that the people's response demonstrates their faith and integrity. The Hebrew term behind "integrity," used in two different forms in 1 Chronicles 29:17, means equity or justice (Psalms 9:8; 58:1; 75:2; 96:10; 98:9; 99:4). "Integrity" is an appropriate translation in some contexts (Deuteronomy 9:5; 1 Kings 9:4), but it mainly refers to doing what is right (thus, "uprightness" in the NRSV). The proper response to God's testing is to do what is right. This "integrity" manifests itself by a willing, joyful gift "with honest intent." The Chronicler intends this as a model of an obedient, grateful response to God's graciousness. God is pleased "with honest intent" (or rightfulness), and thus he is pleased with kings that do what is "right" in their eyes (cf. 2 Chronicles 14:2). The Chronicler teaches his community how to respond graciously to God's grace.

2 Corinthians 8 and 9 is another example of such teaching. Paul tests the integrity and sincerity of the Corinthians' love by exhorting them to give to the poor saints in Jerusalem (2 Corinthians 8:8). His appeal is based upon the grace that God had demonstrated in Jesus Christ (2 Corinthians 8:9). The Corinthians ought to "grace" the poor because God has "graced" them so that "grace" (thanks) might return to God (2 Corinthians 8:1, 4, 6, 7, 9, 16, 19; 9:8, 14, 15).

David prays for the hearts of his people and that of his son (1 Chronicles 28:18-19). His petition calls for God's gracious activity in a human heart. Integrity and uprightness do not simply flow out of human self-resolve. Rather, God works good things in the hearts of his people. The prayer assumes human responsibility, but it also seeks divine activity. Both are complementary and necessary values in God's relationship with his people.

David's petition draws on the covenantal promise of God to "Abraham, Isaac, and Jacob." The children of Jacob are the children of promise; they are the people of God. David claims this relationship and asks God to "keep this desire in" their "hearts" and "keep their hearts loyal" to him. The heart is the crucial area of relationship with God. God seeks committed, "loyal" hearts that yearn for relationship with him. The "desire" refers to the willing, joyful generosity of 1 Chronicles 27:17. David prays that God will prepare their hearts just as he himself has prepared for the temple (1 Chronicles 29:19, "provided").

God gives wealth, and God uses that wealth to test the hearts of his people. Will his people consume their wealth and use it for their own purposes, or will his people share their wealth and scatter it according to divine interests (for the sake of the kingdom and the poor; cf. Psalm 112:9)? Wealth tests the integrity of human hearts. What the people of God do with their wealth demonstrates the character of their hearts and the nature of their commitment to the kingdom of God.

TESTING THE POWERFUL

The narrative of the kings of Judah in 2 Chronicles 10-36 is punctuated with assessments of whether the kings do "what is right" in the eyes of the Lord (cf. 2 Chronicles 14:2; 20:32; 24:2; 25:2; 26:4; 27:2; 28:1; 29:2, 34; 31:20; 34:2). As noted above, David praised God as one who tests the heart and is "pleased with integrity" (i.e., those who do what is "right"). The function of the royal narratives is to unveil the heart of Judah's kings. In particular, God tests the powerful to see whether or not they seek the Lord from the heart. The reign of Asa is a good example of this sort of testing (2 Chronicles 14-16).

TESTING THE PEACE OF ASA'S REIGN

The reign of Asa, at least the first ten years, was a time of spiritual renewal under a "good" king who did what was "right in the eyes of the Lord his God" (2 Chronicles 14:2). He led a religious reform movement which "removed the high places and incense altars in every town in Judah" along with "foreign altars, sacred stones," and "Asherah poles" (2 Chronicles 14:3, 5). He stripped Judah of its idolatrous practices and directed

"Judah to seek the Lord" and "to obey his laws and commands." Torah piety is the center of Asa's reform movement.

God blessed Asa and Judah with peace because they "sought the Lord" (2 Chronicles 14:7). But the blessing of peace is threatened by an invasion from the south. Why is this peace interrupted with war? While such a turn of events might be generally construed in Chronicles as a punishment, there is nothing in the text to suggest that here. On the contrary, it appears that the invasion is a test of Asa's (and Judah's) commitment to seek the Lord. The test is whether they will seek the Lord in the face of an invading army or whether they will seek another resource (e.g., an alliance with a neighboring nation).

Significantly, Zerah the Cushite (Nubian, which is near modern Sudan; 2 Chronicles 14:9) led this Egyptian invasion. While Pharoah Shishak invaded Judah as a punishment during the reign of Rehoboam (2 Chronicles 12:1-11), this Egyptian invasion comes on the heels of spiritual renewal as a test of Judah's commitment to seek the Lord.

The invasion force reaches Mareshah, which is located west of Hebron just to the north of Lachish, within forty miles of Jerusalem. God permitted this invading force to reach deep within the state of Judah. Zerah's army was numbered at one million, while Asa's Judean army was only half that size. The contrast (2 to 1) emphasizes the powerless position in which Asa found himself before an invading army. The question now is: whom will Asa trust? Asa turns to God and prays:

> Lord, there is no one like you to help the powerless against the mighty. Help us, O Lord our God, for we rely on you, and in your name we have come against this vast army. O Lord, you are our God; do not let man prevail against you. (2 Chronicles 14:11)His prayer moves from confession ("there is no one like you")

73

through petition ("help us") to confidence ("do not let man prevail against you"). Asa confesses that God alone is able "to help the powerless against the mighty." This expresses utter dependence on God who holds the victory in his hands. God is sovereign over this battle—he will give victory to whomever he desires. Asa, through faith, relied on God. While Asa's piety did not exclude him from the possibility of crisis, he bore witness to the victory of faith as he relied on God. War invaded Judah during a time of peace and blessing. God tested the faith of Judah. Faith won the victory because faith relied on a faithful, sovereign God.

In the wake of the victory, God sends a prophet to interpret His actions (2 Chronicles 15:1-8) and Judah responds with a covenant renewal festival (2 Chronicles 15:9-15). God acted to redeem his people, and the prophet explained the significance of the victory. The people, in grateful response, celebrate the victory and renew their covenant with God.

The fundamental message is that if Judah will seek the Lord, the Lord will find them, but if they forsake him, he will forsake them (2 Chronicles 15:2). The center of the text is 2 Chronicles 15:12-14. The people "entered into a covenant to seek the Lord, the God of their fathers, with all their heart and soul." This language is the essence of faithfulness— seeking the Lord with the whole heart (cf. Deuteronomy 6:5; Matthew 22:37).

The concluding note (2 Chronicles 15:15) stresses the faithfulness of God. Judah "sought" God and he was "found" by them. Judah dedicated its whole heart to God through swearing a covenantal oath to him, and God blessed Judah with "rest." God is faithful; he is with those who are with him.

TESTING THE PEACE OF ASA'S VICTORY

Up to this point, Asa is portrayed as a pious king who leads a faithful Judah, but in a subsequent distressful situation with Baasha, the king of Israel, Asa relies on the king of Aram. In 2 Chronicles 16:1-10, Asa forfeits the peace with which he has been blessed. Instead of seeking God for help, he seeks help from the king of Aram.

While Judah was enjoying the divine blessing of peace, Baasha, king of Israel, "fortified Rama" in the territory of Benjamin only five miles north of Jerusalem (2 Chronicles 16:1). God permitted this invasion, just as he permitted Zerah to invade, in order to test Asa's heart. Will Judah seek God or someone else?

Unfortunately, as Asa faces Baasha's relatively weak, hostile act, he does not rely on God. Rather, he seeks a foreign alliance. He trusts Ben-Hadad rather than having faith in the Lord. Instead of relying on God's covenant with David, Asa relies on his family's covenant with Ben-Hadad.

Asa's move is successful (2 Chronicles 16:4-6), but when Judah returns from fortifying Geba and Mizpah, a prophet condemns Asa (2 Chronicles 16:7-9). What had appeared a success was actually a failure.

The prophetic speech to Asa has three points. First, Asa sees the immediate problem but cannot see Yahweh's potential. The prophet proclaims to him, "if you had relied" on Yahweh, God would have given not only Baasha but also the "king of Aram" into "your hand." Asa's problem limited his vision. If he had sought the Lord, God would have given him the whole land of Israel, including the regions of Syria. Second, the prophet reminds Asa of his previous faith and how God redeemed Judah from the hand of the Egyptians. Whereas Asa relied on God in his battle with Zerah in 2 Chronicles 14:11 (cf. 2 Chronicles 13:18), here Asa relies on the king of Syria. Third, the prophet announces Asa's punishment. His "foolish" act means that "from now on you will be at war."

In support of the second point, the Chronicler articulates a vision of God that is significant for understanding the basic theme of Chronicles: God seeks seekers. God delivers those who seek him because "the eyes of the Lord range throughout the earth to strengthen those whose hearts are fully committed to him" (2 Chronicles 16:9). God searches the earth and, by his watchful presence, is ready to help those who trust him. God, a seeker himself (1 Chronicles 28:9), takes notice and acts to help those who seek him. Had Asa kept his heart dedicated to God, he would have found God and the strength to resist Baasha. God actively engages the world to find those who seek him. We can have confidence knowing that, as we seek God, he will strengthen us for the task he has given us.

Asa's response to the prophet is the opposite of his reaction to Azariah in 2 Chronicles 15:8. Instead of submitting to the word of the Lord, Asa is angered and rejects the prophetic message. He imprisons the prophet and begins a brutal oppression of the people. Asa's faithlessness likens him to Rehoboam who also oppressed Israel. Even worse, though Rehoboam submitted to the prophet in 2 Chronicles 11: 1-3, Asa persecutes the prophet. Asa's anger against the prophet also turned against God's people. Asa's pride in his own accomplishment (the defeat of Baasha) blinds him from seeing his own sin.

Despite Asa's heart failures with Baasha and his foot disease, his "heart was fully committed [to the Lord] all his life" (2 Chronicles 15:17). But how does one square "all his life" with the stories in 2 Chronicles 16 where Asa fails to rely fully on God? Theologically, even when the heart is fully dedicated to God, there are moments of weakness that result in moral failure. Nevertheless, God accepts the heart even with its failures. The Chronicler emphasizes the dynamic relationship between God and his people: "if you seek the Lord, he will be found; and if you forsake him, he will forsake you." Asa illustrates both the first and the last. When Asa sought the Lord, he won a peace, but when he forsook the Lord, he lost the peace. Nevertheless, when God looks at his life as a whole, he sees a king who does what is "right" and his "heart" is committed to God. Moral weakness, even failures in relation to the specific testing of God, do not undermine God's gracious consideration of a heart that is oriented toward him.

Conclusion

God is dynamically involved in testing the wealthy and powerful. He blesses some with power and wealth, but he also holds them accountable for how they use that blessing. God seeks hearts that do what is "right." God seeks integrity and tests the heart to reveal whether the powerful and wealthy trust him or whether they trust their power and wealth.

The call for social justice is a test for the powerful and wealthy. Will the rich share their wealth with the needy and use it for the sake of the kingdom of God? Will the powerful use their status and position to assist the weak and promote the values of the kingdom of God? Or, will the rich consume their wealth on luxury and the powerful advance only themselves?

God tests the hearts of the wealthy and powerful. He calls

the wealthy to share with the poor and the powerful to use their might for redemptive purposes. As Christians who live in a wealthy and powerful nation, we must remember that God is still testing his people. Will we use our wealth and power toward the goal of social justice as it serves the values of the kingdom, or will we consume our wealth and use our power for our own egotistical or nationalistic purposes? The jury, which is the whole of creation, watches to see what Americans will do with their wealth and power.

6   Justice & Inclusiveness

John Mark Hicks

Chronicles is perhaps best known for its emphases on genealogies, ritual details, and immediate retribution. The Chronicler is often portrayed as a harsh legalist who has no mercy for those who violate the parameters of ritualistic purity. But actually he narrates the story of a merciful and inclusive God.

The Ahaz narrative (2 Chronicles 28) highlights God's compassion for his people, even in the depths of their sin. Despite their abject apostasy, God called Israel to show Judah mercy and compassion in the aftermath of a battle. "Samaritan" Israel acted compassionately toward their enemy, Judah, because of God's own compassion for his people.

The Hezekiah narrative (2 Chronicles 30) highlights God's inclusiveness as he called "Samaritan" Israel to celebrate the Passover in Jerusalem. Despite the apostasy of the northern kingdom, God still sought a restored relationship with them. This inclusiveness transcended ritualistic and ethnic boundaries as the mercy of God overflowed for his people.

The Chronicler then narrates two stories that articulate two central values of a divine ethic of social justice: compassion (mercy) and inclusiveness. The Chronicler, a narrative theologian of grace, teaches the postexilic community to show compassion to "Samaritans" and include their lost brothers (as well as aliens) in the restored community.

"SAMARITAN" COMPASSION (2 CHRONICLES 28)

Israel Defeats Judah. Ahaz represents extreme degeneration in Judah. Ahaz embraced idolatry and undermined the temple cultus. Ahaz "did not do what was right in the eyes of the Lord" (2 Chronicles 28:1), and he epitomizes the evil that ultimately results in the exile.

The divine punishment for sin (2 Chronicles 28:5-21) is bounded on either side by the sins of Ahaz (2 Chronicles 28:2-4, 22-25). Thus, the apostasy provides the rationale for Judah's defeat and captivity (their "mini-exile"). The punishment of Judah involves the loss of territory, people (death and captivity), and economic resources. The resultant Judah is a small, poor, and defenseless nation. The sin of Ahaz has destroyed the almost Solomonic glory of his grandfather Uzziah's kingdom (cf. 2 Chronicles 26).

This national condition parallels Judah's postexilic status as a small, poor, Persian province. The postexilic community can also identify with Hezekiah's renewal in 2 Chronicles 29-31. While despair may overwhelm the postexilic community, Chronicles offers hope through a renewal that is grounded in the faithfulness of God.

Aram and Israel invade Judah "because Judah had forsaken the Lord, the God of their fathers" (2 Chronicles 28:6). The key term is "forsake," the Chronicler's word for apostasy (cf. 1 Chronicles 28:9). Whoever forsakes God will be forsaken by him. Both nations took "prisoners" to their home capitals as Judah experienced a mini-exile.

Israel Shows Mercy. Obed, a "prophet of the Lord," confronts the returning army of Israel in Samaria (2 Chronicles 28:9b-11). Obed contrasts what God has done with what Israel has done. God gave Israel victory over Judah, but Israel abused their victory. They exceeded their proper role in God's punishment. Israel should have been restrained by their own sense of guilt before God and by their own cry for mercy against Assyria. Only the merciful receive mercy (Matthew 5:7; James 2:13).

Their guilt, vengeance, greed, and bloodthirstiness emboldened Israel to enslave their brothers and sisters. By enslaving their kinsmen, they violated Torah (cf. Leviticus 25:42-46). Nehemiah 5:5 uses the same words ("subdue slaves") to describe the situation of some families in the postexilic community. The Chronicler rebukes those in his own community who are enslaving kinsmen for economic profit. They must return their "fellow countrymen" (literally, brothers) to their rightful home. The text rebukes the social injustice of the postexilic community as well as narrating the injustice of Israel's action against Judah. The "leaders" reinforce the prophetic message: to enslave Judah is to bring even more guilt upon Israel.

The speeches of Obed and the Ephraimite leaders in 2 Chronicles 28 indicate that the Chronicler believed that both north and south were heirs to the divine promises. The Chronicler did not view northern Israelites as outsiders but as brothers to be reclaimed and reincorporated into the religious and political life of Jerusalem. Postexilic Judah, therefore, must be inclusive and seek out northern believers. The north is not finally and irrevocably rejected. Grace and forgiveness are as open to them as they are to southern believers.

Israel obeys Obed and their leaders (2 Chronicles 28:14-15). They collect all their booty (in men and spoils) and present it "in the presence of the officials and all the assembly." A committee returned the spoils to Judah. They "clothed all who were naked, provided them clothes and sandals, food and drink, and healing balm." They carried the "weak" on "donkeys." They returned the Judahites to their "countrymen ('brothers') at Jericho." The oasis of Jericho is an appropriate symbol as the returning exiles find refreshment at the place where Israel first entered the land of promise.

The northerners "are described as complying with Yahweh's will not because they came to the Temple to worship, but because they freed the captive, fed the hungry, watered the thirsty, and clothed the naked" (cf. Isaiah 58:7; Ezekiel 18:5-9).[44] The northerners imitated the God of Israel (Deuteronomy 29:4; Psalm 146:7-8). Chronicles, of course, invites them to participate in the temple (cf. 2 Chronicles 30), but the fundamental value is the imitation of God. They treated their brothers (neighbors) in the way God would treat them. This is the highest value for Chronicles as Israel manifests the heart of God. This is the ethic of Jesus as well (cf. Matthew 25:31-46), where mercy, justice, and faithfulness are the supreme values (cf. Matthew 23:23).

SAMARITAN MERCY

Spencer notes the similarities between this narrative and the parable of the Good Samaritan (Luke 10:25-37).[45] Both storylines involve Jews who were stripped, beaten, and robbed. Both involve northern Israelites (Samaritans) who anointed, clothed, and transported the injured to Jericho. Both are obedient to Leviticus 19:17-18, where Israel is told to love their neighbors and abstain from hating their brothers. They differ, however, concerning the role of the leaders. While the leaders in Jesus' parable ignore the injured man when they are expected to help, the leaders of Israel persuade the attackers to help the injured. The leaders of Israel in Chronicles manifest a love for their brothers that the priest and Levite of the parable did not. "Essentially," Spencer writes, the Chronicler, "Jesus, and Luke represent an unbroken chain of prophets calling for loving unity among the people of God, unfettered by social discrimination."[46]

The significance for the postexilic community is important. The mercy of the northern Israelites, which embraced "brotherhood" with the south, is a model for how postexilic Judah should treat northern Israelites who seek God. This mercy is rooted in the love of brother/neighbor (Leviticus 19:15-18).

The very thing the leaders of Israel feared (2 Chronicles 28:9-13), Ahaz discounted. By turning to "other gods," Ahaz "provoked the Lord, the God of his fathers, to anger." Israel, in this circumstance, was more faithful than the son of David. The kingdom that had rejected David in 1 Chronicles 10 and 1 Chronicles 13 showed mercy to David's descendents out of respect for Yahweh.

THE INCLUSION OF "SAMARITANS"

With the northern kingdom now in exile and only the southern kingdom continuing, opportunity arrives. Although the north has experienced the judgment of God, the Davidic kingdom with its temple offers northerners hope. Hezekiah, therefore, speaks in a conciliatory manner. His speech invites the north to participate in the worship of Yahweh at the Jerusalem temple (2 Chronicles 30:6b-9).

Hezekiah's speech to a judged nation addresses the Chronicler's own postexilic community. All Israel (north and south) are invited to the temple to worship Yahweh. Whether it is the judged northern kingdom in Assyrian exile or the judged southern kingdom in Babylonian exile, the restored community in postexilic Jerusalem invites all Israel to seek Yahweh.

THE PASSOVER PLANNED (2 CHRONICLES 30:1-4)

The heart of the Chronicler's account of Hezekiah's Passover is theological (2 Chronicles 30). The celebration of the Passover remembers the Exodus, emulates the arrival of the ark into Jerusalem in 1 Chronicles 13, 15-16, re-lives the two-week celebration of the temple dedication by Solomon (2 Chronicles 7), and celebrates the reunion of north and south at the temple. As Williamson demonstrates, the Chronicler employs the language of 2 Chronicles 7:14 to highlight this moment of national repentance. [47] Just as God promised Solomon (2 Chronicles 7:14), if Israel will "humble" themselves (2 Chronicles 30:11), "pray" (2 Chronicles 30:18), "seek" (2 Chronicles 30:19), and "turn" (2 Chronicles 30:9), God will "hear" (2 Chronicles 30:20) and "heal" (2 Chronicles 30:20).

Theologically, Hezekiah's Passover was the first recorded Passover since the schism to encompass both Israel and Judah. Thus, it had both Davidic and Solomonic proportions as all Israel celebrated God's redemptive grace. Worship is a time of unity, thankful remembrance, and seeking God's face. In short, "it is a time for the reorientation of the human heart—to remember what God has done in the past and to infuse the present with hope for a future life of well-being and communion with God."[48]

Hezekiah intends a national celebration that includes "all Israel and Judah" (2 Chronicles 30:1). Hezekiah models an attitude that the postexilic community must also embrace—inclusiveness. They must welcome their northern relatives to the Jerusalem temple.

The Passover should be celebrated on the fourteenth day of the first month, but the whole nation decided to celebrate it in "the second month." Most believe Chronicles assumes the "Second Passover" law of Numbers 9:2-14 as the explanation for the month delay. This law permits those who are unclean at the time of the first month to celebrate the Passover in the second month once they are clean. Hezekiah's temple and nation were unclean on the fourteenth day of the first month and thus could not celebrate the Passover. Hezekiah, therefore, extends the individual legislation of Numbers 9 to a national level. The whole nation will celebrate the Passover in the second month rather than the first.

Chronicles is defensive about the date and recognizes that it is irregular. The rationale provided in 2 Chronicles 30:3 is two-fold. First, "not enough priests had consecrated themselves" for the celebration. During the dedication rites the Levites had to assist the priests in the sacrificial ritual because there were too few of them (2 Chronicles 29:34). Second, the people were not yet "assembled in Jerusalem." The temple cleansing had taken the first half of the first month to complete and once it was complete there was not enough time to assemble the people for a pilgrimage festival in Jerusalem.

The Chronicler's rationale for the irregularity does not invoke Numbers 9 and his rationale includes more than Numbers 9 explicitly permits. Numbers 9 permits a second

Passover but it does not permit a wholesale abrogation of the first. For Chronicles, it was not the uncleanness of the people that permitted the cancellation of the first Passover date, but the insufficient number of consecrated priests and the inability to gather the people in Jerusalem so quickly. These exigencies permitted a new Passover date so that it could be celebrated in that calendar year.[49] Thus, for Chronicles, the gracious renewal of fellowship with God is more important than the particulars of the Passover date. Mercy takes precedence over sacrifice; or grace takes precedence over ritual (cf. Hosea 6:6; Matthew 9:13; 12:7). The law of Numbers 9 is itself a reflection of God's merciful intention rather than his unyielding demand for ritualistic perfection. Thus, the Chronicler is no extreme ritualistic or perfectionistic legalist.

The Invitation to Northern Israel (30:6-9)

The letter, primarily addressed to the northern tribes (literally, "children of Israel"), articulates the guiding principle in its opening and closing. The use of the verb "return" forms an *inclusio* for the letter and occurs six times. God will return to them and return ("come back") their exiled brothers to their land if they all will return ("turn") to him. This expresses the fundamental theological principle of Chronicles (1 Chronicles 28:9; 2 Chronicles 7:14-22; 15:2): God seeks the seekers, and the seekers find God. Further, the call to "return" is inherent in the character of God, which is the hope of God's people, because "the Lord your God is gracious and compassionate" (the only time these two words occur together in Chronicles; cf. Exodus 34:6; Psalm 86:15; 103:8; 111:4; 145:8). God is faithful and "he will not turn his face from you if you return to him." Thus, this principle expresses the relational and gracious heart of God.

The negative imperatives remind the northerners of their past. Their ancestors did not seek the Lord, but rather they were "unfaithful" (cf. 2 Chronicles 9:1) and "stiff-necked" (cf. 2 Chronicles 36:13). Consequently, God "made them an object of horror" and God turned his "anger" on them (cf. 2 Chronicles 29:8). The letter does not stand arrogantly over Israel, but rather Judah stands alongside of Israel as a fellow-sufferer of God's anger. They both have been made a "horror" and both have suffered God's "anger." They both have been "unfaithful" (cf. 2 Chronicles 29:6). One fallen brother reaches out to another. The letter invites Israel to join Judah in their return to God.

The positive imperatives ("submit," "come," and "serve") build on each other. "Submit" is literally "give the hand" (cf. 1 Chronicles 29:24), which is a pledge of loyalty. God seeks a humble heart that submits. Second, Israel is invited to come to the sanctified "sanctuary" which God has given to his people "forever." Coming to the sanctuary is coming to God and embracing his faithfulness. Third, they should "serve the Lord." In this context, "serve" has a liturgical meaning. The invitation is for Israel to offer their loyalty to the Lord, to come to his temple, and to worship him. These constitutes "returning" to God.

The theological message for the postexilic community is two-fold. First, it is in the same situation as the northern kingdom. It is a remnant that survived the Babylonian assaults and exile. The principle, "'if you return to the Lord,' then God will return to you," speaks to them. The postexilic community should embrace the hope rooted in God's faithfulness to his people and his gracious intent toward them. Second, the postexilic community should offer a similar letter to their northern neighbors. The principle applies as much to the north in 400 B.C. as it did in 715 B.C. God yearns for the reunion of his people in his holy presence. The Babylonian remnant must accept the Assyrian remnant. Brother must accept brother, as the faithfulness of God demands (cf. Romans 15:5-7).

RITUALISTIC IRREGULARITIES

While the temple and clergy have been sanctified, "many in the crowd had not consecrated themselves" (2 Chronicles 30:17). Consequently, they could not kill their own animals. Due to their uncleanness, "the Levites had to kill the Passover lambs" for them. Unclean people cannot kill consecrated lambs. Chronicles demonstrates a concern for cultic ritual by noting the substitution of the "Levites" for the worshippers in this case.

But may unclean people eat the Passover? The text clearly indicates that they did. Unclean people, especially "many people who came from Ephraim, Manasseh, Issachar and Zebulun," ate what was clean. This is a clear violation of the Law of Moses. 2 Chronicles 30:19 explicitly notes that they "ate the Passover contrary to what was written."

Some have invoked Numbers 9 as a specific authorization for unclean people to eat the Passover. But Numbers 9 does not address this situation. Eves argues:

> The original intent of the Numbers passage is to allow those who are unclean at the time of the Passover feast to be ceremonially clean by the Second Passover and able to keep it. However, the working assumption of the passage is that at the time of the Second Passover they will be culticly clean. To a considerable degree, however, this is not the case concerning Hezekiah's Passover. Incredibly, another

ingenious alteration (if not rejection) of the Numbers legislation is that Hezekiah knowingly allows unclean people to eat the Passover. (2 Chronicles 20:17, 18) [50]

The issue in Numbers 9 is not whether or not unclean people may eat the Passover; the presumption of Numbers 9 is that those who eat a "second Passover" will be clean when they eat it. Numbers 9 does not authorize unclean people to eat the Passover. 2 Chronicles 20:18 violates even Numbers 9 and explicitly violates Leviticus 7:19-21 regarding sacrificial meals, which includes the Passover.

Why was this cultic violation not punished with death, as in the case of Uzzah in 1 Chronicles 13, or Uzziah in 2 Chronicles 26, or even Nadab and Abihu in Leviticus 10? Hezekiah's prayer answers the question and reveals the essence of the Chronicler's theology of worship. Uzzah was part of an unholy convocation, and he dared to touch the presence of God (cf. 1 Chronicles 13).[51] Uzziah is condemned for his pride, rather than for the technicality of ritual violations (2 Chronicles 26:16). Nadab and Abihu rebelliously, and in their drunkenness, contradicted the command of God by taking fire from a place other than God prescribed (cf. Leviticus 10). Hezekiah acts on the principle that God cares more about the heart than ritualistic technicalities.

Hezekiah's prayer appeals to the gracious promise of God in 2 Chronicles 6-7 (especially 2 Chronicles 7:14). The critical point is the orientation of the person, the one "who sets his heart on seeking God." This phrase combines two extremely important words in Chronicles: "heart" and "seeking." Hezekiah prays for the forgiveness of those who violated the divine ritual out of a heart that sought God. The guiding principle of forgiveness is two-fold: (1) the goodness of God who seeks a people for himself (1 Chronicles 28:9; 29:14-17) and (2) the orientation of the heart toward God. God forgives those who seek him even when they violate his cultic legislations. This is the principle of mercy over sacrifice (Hosea 6:6; Matthew 9:13; 12:7).

God accepted unclean worshippers because they had a heart to seek him. The text explicitly records, as if to emphasize the legitimacy of Hezekiah's request, that "the Lord heard Hezekiah and healed the people" (which is the promise of 2 Chronicles 7:14). 2 Chronicles 30:18-20 clarifies that 2 Chronicles 7:14 is not to be interpreted culticly, but according to the heart. The ritual is not the most important thing. Even the Sabbath, with all its strict regulations and penalties, was secondary to human needs and suffering. The Sabbath was made for humanity, not humanity for the Sabbath (cf. Mark 2:23-3:6). Ritual is made for humanity, not humanity for ritual. Rituals serve the ends for which God has designed them, but they must never be used to oppress and repress the heart that seeks God.

The Inclusiveness

The enthusiasm of the joyous celebration of the Passover in 2 Chronicles 30:21-22 overflows into the extension of the celebration for an additional week, even though there is no precedent in the Law of Moses for such an extension.

The roll call of participants in 2 Chronicles 30:25 highlights several important groups: (1) "entire assembly of Judah"; (2) "priests and Levites"; (3) "all who had assembled from Israel;" and (4) "aliens who had come from Israel and those who lived in Judah." The inclusiveness of this list is apparent. Not only were northern Israelites free to come to the festival but also "aliens" in the land. Theologically, this use of "alien" connects with David's prayer in 1 Chronicles 29:15. Israel is itself an alien in the earth, but nonetheless blessed by God. So also Israel as an alien must receive the aliens in her midst (cf. Exodus 12:48-49). The participation of the aliens fulfills part of the mission of Israel to serve the nations and bear witness to the light of God.

The theological interest for the postexilic community is how they will imitate their ancestors. Will they seek the Lord by including their northern brothers? This is a rallying cry for the people of God. Whoever seeks the Lord, let them submit, come, and worship him (2 Chronicles 30:8). God accepts everyone who seeks him, even when they seek him through prescribed rituals imperfectly.

Conclusion

The demands of social justice include mercy and compassion. Chronicles calls its original readers to extend mercy to their "separated brothers," even in their ritual impurity. Restored Judah must include not only Israel ("Samaritans"), but also the aliens in the land. Restored Judah must practice the values of mercy, compassion, and inclusiveness as the embodiment of the kingdom of God on earth.

The kingdom of God is present in the ministry of Jesus who continues and exegetes these values. The life and teaching of Jesus, who prefers mercy over sacrifice and offers redemption (and table fellowship) to all, no matter what their social, economic, or ethnic status, embodies the values of Israel's God. Social justice is a kingdom value, and just as the Chronicler called Judah to practice divine justice and mercy, so the kingdom of God today is called to follow those same values, especially as they are articulated and practiced in the life of Jesus.

Sermon on the Mount

7 Justice & the Coming of the Kingdom

Lee Camp

Many take the assignment of speaking on "The Sermon on the Mount and Social Justice" as missing the very point of the Sermon on the Mount: Jesus is not describing here, commentators and theologians suggest, an ethic that is to be taken seriously in the "real world" of injustice, of scarcity, of oppression, or of violence. For some, Jesus merely describes a lovely "ideal" world—and this "ideal" may provide, for example, the realization that we are all sinners and thus stand in need of God's gracious pardon in order for us to "make it to heaven." Therefore, it is argued, the Sermon (or other of Jesus' teachings) does not provide any "real" guidance in the "real" world.

For others, the Sermon on the Mount informs our *attitudes*, but not our actions. If we "turn the other cheek," how can there be "justice"? And so, it is concluded, we are not to "love our enemies" in any concrete sense, but in our "heart." For yet others, the Sermon provides an ethical matrix for use in the realm of the "personal," but not in the realm of the "social" or "political." Jesus came proclaiming a kingdom that is "spiritual," but not "political" or "social," it is suggested, and thus the Sermon on the Mount does not provide any sort of concrete ethical guidance for those seeking to foster social justice in our real-world communities.

THE KINGDOM IN THE SERMON ON THE MOUNT

In this and other ways, the teaching of Jesus is systematically set aside; in thoughtful, nuanced ways, many compartmentalize, trivialize, or otherwise reduce his authority as Lord of Lords. Here I suggest that if we take into account both the immediate context and the larger canonical context as a whole, we discover Jesus proclaiming a very realistic and creative lifestyle by which we might simultaneously respond to injustice and bear faithful witness to the Kingdom of Heaven.

The incipient Marcionism that undergirds much of our reading of the New Testament can cause us to miss the very crucial theological claim that makes the Sermon on the Mount relevant to social justice. That is, a great level of change and discontinuity is assumed between the Old and New Testaments: the Old Testament was about Law, the New Testament about grace; the Old Testament depicts a warring, legalistic God, while the New Testament pictures a God of love and mercy; the Old Testament has Moses, the New Testament, Jesus; the Old Testament pertains to this-worldly theocracies, the New Testament to an other-worldly kingdom. All these assumptions lead us to suppose a discontinuity between the teaching of Jesus and that of the Old Law.

One need not settle, however, all the questions of Matthew's understanding of the relation between Jesus and the Old Law to see the great importance of the *continuity* that makes the Sermon relevant to issues of social justice. This continuity provides the key to understanding the Sermon

Or as it was put in one of the lament psalms, "God, why don't you just wake up and come do something?" (my paraphrase of Psalm 44:23).

JESUS AND THE KINGDOM

In the midst of such cries, Jesus appears: "the kingdom of heaven is at hand!" We miss the significance of "fulfillment" language in Matthew if we merely restrict the meaning of "fulfilled" to the "fulfillment of predictive prophecy." Much more, Matthew depicts Jesus as the fulfillment of the long awaited purposes of God. The day of justice, righteousness, and peace was dawning. So Jesus' proclamation of the coming Kingdom while he wandered throughout the region of Zebulun and Naphtali, Matthew declares, is the fulfillment of the words of Isaiah:

Land of Zebulun, land of Naphtali,
On the road by the sea, across the Jordan,
   Galilee of the Gentiles —
The people who sat in darkness have seen a great light,
And for those who sat in the region and shadow of death,
   light has dawned.
(Matthew 4:15-16; cf. Isaiah. 9:1-2)

Jesus' proclamation thus stands as the culmination of the prophetic longing for the will of God to triumph in human affairs, a this-worldly reality that Matthew describes as the "kingdom of heaven."

The context of Matthew's fulfillment oracle is instructive. Isaiah 9 describes the appearance of the light of God in conjunction with an end to the injustice and violence that destroy communities and peoples:

For all the boots of the tramping warriors
And all the garments rolled in blood
Shall be burned as fuel for the fire.
For a child has been born for us,
A son given to us;
Authority rests upon his shoulders;
And he is named
Wonderful Counselor, Mighty God,
Everlasting Father, Prince of Peace. (Isaiah 9:5f.)

This one who is coming shall establish an
authority in which there will be
Endless peace for the throne of David and his kingdom.
He will establish and uphold it
With justice and with righteousness
From this time onward and forevermore. (Isaiah 9:7)

Our notion of "Christ," though, often misses the role of bringing about justice and righteousness in real historical communities. We often take "Christ" as merely a name, Jesus' surname, "Jesus Christ." Or alternately, "Christ" is thought to be a designation regarding the metaphysical nature of Jesus, as both God and Man. But the prophetic vision of the coming One, the Anointed One, sets forth a vision of one who judges rightly, not giving preferential treatment: "But with righteousness he shall judge the poor, / and decide with equity for the meek of the earth" (Isaiah 11:4a). In other words, our notion of "Christ" as merely the one who provides the religious sacrifice necessary for the primarily after-life reward of heaven misses the biblical connotation of "Messiah."

The Prophets, along with the Old Testament lament literature, repeatedly raise the question of "where is God?" In the midst of injustice, the Prophets long for the coming of the God of justice; in the midst of unfaithfulness, the Prophets anticipate the vindicated promises of the God who is faithful; in the midst of poverty, the Prophets long for the abundance of the Messianic banquet; in the midst of oppression, the Prophets long for the God who delivered Hebrew slaves from Egypt. The "good news" announced by Jesus is that this long-awaited Day of God's Rule had appeared.

Much Old Testament and intertestamental literature anticipates the coming Day in which God will vindicate the righteous, and destroy the wicked. "He shall strike the earth with the rod of his mouth, / and with the breath of his lips he shall kill the wicked" (Isaiah 11:4b).

With the triumph of the righteous, then, shall come the reversal of the fallen creation. Evil, violence, and injustice will be undone and replaced with the peace and provision that God always intended for his creation. Given that the Genesis account depicts violence as a result of the fall (cf. fratricide in Genesis 4; and Genesis 6:11-13), the coming day of the triumph of God's purposes in human history will be accompanied by a renewal of a primeval peace:

> The wolf shall live with the lamb,
> The leopard shall lie down with the kid,
> The calf and the lion and the fatling together,
> And a little child shall lead them.
> The cow and the bear shall graze,
> Their young shall lie down together;
> And the lion shall eat straw like the ox.
> The nursing child shall play over the hole of the asp,
> And the weaned child shall put its hand on the adder's den.
> They will not hurt or destroy
> On all my holy mountain;
> For the earth will be full of the knowledge of the Lord
> As the waters cover the sea (Isaiah 11:6-9).

Such pictures are indispensable in understanding Jesus' own proclamation of "the kingdom of heaven." Jesus proclaims the presence of the rule and reign of God for which generations had waited; it is now "at hand," or "is near," as Matthew 4:17 is alternately translated. The "kingdom of heaven" is not off in heaven, or something to be known and experienced only in the "sweet by and by," but has come near.

The parallelism employed in the "Lord's Prayer" in the Sermon provides a succinct definition of "kingdom of heaven." "Pray then in this way," Jesus taught:

> Our Father in heaven,
> hallowed be your name.
> Your kingdom come.
> Your will be done,
> on earth as it is in heaven. (Matthew 6:9f)

For God's name to be "hallowed" does not primarily connote not "cursing." Instead, for God's name—God's self— to be "hallowed" connotes that the things for which God stands, the things God has promised, should come to pass. The things in which God is interested—justice, righteousness, and peace—will come to pass in human history and vindicate the name of God. Jesus thus teaches us to call upon God to come be God, to come do the God-stuff God is supposed to do.

So the expression, "hallowed be your name," is almost synonymous with the next phrase: "may your kingdom come." And to pray that God's Kingdom come is synonymous with praying "your will be done, on earth as it is in heaven." Taking this as our cue to the meaning of "kingdom," Jesus' message might be summarized this way: The long-awaited reign of

God over his creation has now come near, located in time, not timelessness; rooted in history, not beyond history; firmly situated in "real-life," not "after-life." It's here—and we pray for its ongoing and ultimate consummation.

Preachers have long castigated the Twelve for misunderstanding the nature of the Kingdom. But perhaps we misunderstand the misunderstanding. Jesus nowhere corrects the twelve or any of his followers for expecting a *this-worldly kingdom*; the difficulty for the Twelve, instead, lay with their expectation of the *manner* and *mode* of the coming of that Kingdom.

The differences between the *expected* mode of the coming of the Kingdom and *Jesus'* mode of the coming Kingdom is nowhere clearer than in the Beatitudes. Robert Schuller's book, *Prescriptions for Happiness*, typifies a spiritualization of the Beatitudes that encourages us to miss this point. Schuller suggests that Jesus' Beatitudes provide certain types of attitudes that will make for "happiness." After all, *makarios* ("blessed") can be translated "happy." But Jesus' Beatitudes provide neither prescriptions for happiness nor positive-thinking characteristics. Neither does Jesus here command these as necessary characteristics of his followers (though Jesus subsequently takes up some of the characteristics described in the Beatitudes and makes them norms for the people of God). Instead, Jesus provides commentary, provides a description of a new reality; those who are "poor in spirit," those who are "meek," those who "mourn," those who "hunger and thirst for righteousness," these are blessed if and only if the rule and reign of God is now at hand.

Consider Matthew 5:4: "Blessed are those who mourn, for they will be comforted." In James 4, believers are commanded to weep, wail, and lament over their sins;

mourning is commanded as a vital component of the practice of repentance. But in the Beatitudes, Jesus appears simply to state a reality: Blessed are they who mourn and grieve over the sins of the world. But *why*? Because the rule of God is now present, in which the injustice, oppression, and repression of the world will be undone. Those who mourn over the sins of the world can now be blessed because the rule of righteousness and justice and peace is now at hand. It is as if in one brief declaration, the whole burden of Jewish lament, the entire load of grief over injustice, the total sum of the tears of God's people are addressed in this simple word of God: the long-awaited rule, the long-awaited reign, the long-awaited vindication is here. Your tears and your grief and your pain have not gone unnoticed—God has heard you, and he is here to bring about his purposes. So, be blessed.

THE UNEXPECTED SHAPE OF THE COMING KINGDOM

But the Beatitudes not only announce the coming of the long-awaited reality of the Kingdom, they also surprise the recipient of this Good News in their description of the nature of the Kingdom's coming. N.T. Wright provides a helpful reading in this vein,[52] insisting that the Sermon be read in light of the contemporary expectations of the social and political shape of the coming Kingdom of God. So he suggests that "blessed are they who mourn" be understood this way: While Israel awaits *paraklesis*, consolation, she must come to realize that God will not give the comfort of nationalistic defeat and punishment of one's enemies, but instead will comfort only those who truly grieve over the sins of the world.

This allows us significant insight, then, into the first beatitude (5:3). While Israel does long for the coming

Kingdom, and is willing to do "whatever it takes" to bring it about, the kingdom comes instead to those who are "poor in spirit," those who do not seek arrogantly to impose themselves, their agendas, or their own self-righteousness over others. This juxtaposition of "poor in spirit" and those who "mourn" gives rise to some observations about different ways we might grieve over the injustices in our world. In the Beatitudes and, indeed, throughout the New Testament, one finds theological trajectories much more in keeping with the theological trajectories of "biblical lament" than what we might call "nationalistic lament." Both in Jesus' day and our own, nationalistic lament was and is alive and well; and nationalistic lament, both in Jesus' day and ours, gives rise to a social and political ethic fundamentally different than that espoused by Jesus.

Out of a misunderstanding of the disciples' misunderstanding, one (rightly, but on wrong premises) concludes that their nationalistic interpretation of the Kingdom was wrong. But if the Kingdom of Heaven was indeed a new social order that had at its heart the correct ordering of the community (which is but another name for "justice"), then we see that what was said to the Jews in their nationalism in the first century can be said to us in our nationalism in our century. Jesus taught that the call for "justice" had to be defined by the ways of God, not the ways of the kingdoms of this world.

Out of this understanding we can fashion two different models for grieving the injustices of our world, one faithful to the Gospel, and one not. Biblical lament, for example, calls upon *God* to rise up and deliver. Nationalistic lament calls upon the nation to rise up and conquer, and asks God's blessings upon us as we do that.[53] The Psalms see God as sovereign, while nationalistic lament is offended at the assault upon the sovereignty of the nation-state. Old Testament lament asks God to bless all peoples with repentance and the righteousness that is from God, while nationalism asks God to bless the nation-state and curse the enemies of the nation-state. Theological lament sees God alone as righteous and all humans as unrighteous, while nationalistic lament sees "our" nation-state as the embodiment of good and any of "our" opponents as the embodiment of evil. The psalmist sees God alone as great, and nationalistic lament sees "our" nation as great.

Because of such human tendency to arrogance, because of the human tendency to focus upon our own agendas rather than the goodness and sovereignty and righteousness of God—who is alone the source of true justice and righteousness and peace—the first Beatitude remains ever relevant: "Blessed are the poor in spirit, for theirs is the kingdom of heaven." That is, we are called to be a people humble before God: not seeing ourselves, our sect, our group, our church, or our nation-state as the righteous ones. God alone is righteous, and we are dependent upon His mercy, strength, provision, and sovereignty.

There follows the blessing upon the "meek" (Matthew 5: 5). Israel indeed longs to "inherit the earth," a hope promised for fulfillment in the Messiah; it will not come through a rod of iron,[54] however, but through the way of meekness, gentleness, and humility. The people of God indeed thirst for justice (Matthew 5:6), but often a thirsting after justice is but another name for hungering for revenge. Jesus thus announces a justice that comes not through warfare but through meekness. The chosen ones likewise desperately hope for mercy, especially that "eschatological mercy of final rescue from her enemies," [55] but it is a mercy promised not to the vengeful but to the merciful (Matthew 5:7). There are those who long to see God (Matthew 5:8), but this will come not through imposing a Pharisaic purity but through a purity of heart. Israel longed to be identified as a son of God, with a nationalistic defeat of her enemies providing overwhelming proof of her status; but Jesus declares that those vindicated as sons are those who emulate the Father. This means not being warmakers but peacemakers (Matthew 5:9). And while the way of Jesus will inevitably result in persecution (Matthew 5:10), vindication is guaranteed.

Wright concludes his helpful description of the meaning of the Beatitudes by saying,

Whatever they have meant to subsequent hearers or readers, I suggest that the Beatitudes can be read, in some such way, as an appeal to Jesus' hearers to discover their true vocation as the eschatological people of YHWH, and to do so by following the praxis he was marking out for them, rather than the way of other would-be leaders of the time. [56]

Put differently, Jesus here called his disciples precisely to a particular social and political ethic, which we might call the "way of the cross." This was not merely a set of attitudes that provide happiness, or an ethic for individuals in dealing with difficult personal relations, but a way of life for the "eschatological people of YHWH." It is a way of life that only makes sense, and is only possible, if indeed the kingdom rule of God has now broken into human history.

The coming Kingdom therefore provides the foundation that makes Jesus' pronouncements in the Sermon possible. Those who have faith that his word is true — that the Kingdom of heaven is now present, in our midst — these can receive his words and obey. Those who do not obey, although they may think themselves being "realistic" or "practical" or "sensible," actually only keep themselves busy with their limited agendas on a sinking ship. Jesus described this non-intuitive reality this way:

Everyone then who hears these words of mine and acts on them will be like a wise man who built his house on rock. The rain fell, the floods came, and the winds blew and beat on that house, but it did not fall, because it had been founded on rock. And everyone who hears these words of mine and does not act on them will be like a foolish man who built his house on sand. The rain fell, and the floods came, and the winds blew and beat against that house, and it fell—and great was its fall! (Matthew 7:24-27)

8   Justice & Non-Violence

Lee Camp

A reading such as that suggested in the previous chapter inevitably brings one to embrace an ethic of non-violence: if the Sermon on the Mount describes the contours of the now-present-and-coming Kingdom of heaven, then the way of Jesus prescribes the way of Kingdom people. The Gospels proclaim that the crucified Messiah reveals a new social order, and thus the way of Jesus—the way of mercy, loving one's enemies, praying for those who despitefully use you—this is the way in which disciples are called to address the injustices propagated by those kingdoms and individuals not yet submissive to the rule of God.

PACIFISM, NOT PASSIVITY

One should be careful not to conclude that "Christian pacifism" is supported only by a few proof-texts in the Sermon on the Mount. Indeed, precisely because of this misconception, the Sermon on the Mount is strategically a very poor place to begin in order to articulate a theology of Christian non-violence. Instead, the entire New Testament bears witness to the way of the cross as the fundamental commitment

109

and shape of the Christian social ethic. Crucifixion and resurrection, a willingness to suffer, and a confidence that God will vindicate—these are the recurring themes of a New Testament ethic. Just a few examples must here suffice. The Gospel of Mark depicts a Jesus who refuses to employ the form of authority employed by "Gentiles," in which authority is "lorded" over others; Jesus instead takes up the way of Suffering Servanthood, calling his disciples to go in the same way. Paul requires of disciples the way of the cross in response to enemies in Romans 12. 1 Peter commends the example of Jesus in his own suffering as the way of the believer. Revelation concludes with a picture of grandiose defeat and destruction of the enemies of God, but the controlling metaphor for the destruction of God's enemies is the slaughtered Lamb that dominates the heavenly scene.

Similarly, the Sermon on the Mount certainly plays a part in a theology of Christian non-violence. Unfortunately, many have misunderstood the Sermon on the Mount to advocate *passivity* to injustice. This faulty interpretation has, in turn, led many simply to discount the Sermon as having any relevance for matters of social justice. So what *does* the Sermon suggest?

A few reflections on yet one other beatitude will provide a beginning point for answering this question: "Blessed are the peacemakers, for they will be called children of God" (5:9). In Jesus' day, as in ours, there were numerous options for being a peacemaker; there were a number of locatable, discernible socio-political options to seek to bring about the justice and righteousness desired by God. Concerning the designation "peacemaker," perhaps many would have immediately thought of Caesar—Caesar was the "peacemaker." Caesar was the one who brought the "Pax Romana," the peace of Rome.[57] Caesar brought peace through superpower threat, through a sheer exercise of power. "You want to mess with us? You want to wake the sleeping giant? We'll destroy you"—this was the method of Caesar. Caesar did, indeed, bring about a certain kind of "peace," an absence of ongoing warfare, because the threat of warfare was squelched by the sheer power of Rome.

There were few Jews in Jesus' day who liked Roman rule; nonetheless some Jews sought, with all good intentions, to work within that bad system to effect positive change. The Herodians, the Sadducees—each party in its own way accepted the evils of Roman rule over Palestine, but worked within the system to bring as much good as possible out of a bad situation. Sure, the system was corrupted, pouring out injustices upon the people of God; but they made the best of it and sought to make small changes from the top-down. Accommodation for the sake of survival of the 'good guys'—this appears to have been the way of the Herodians and Saduccees.

Others were much more concerned with their own ritual holiness, purity, and the Law of God. They would not be found getting *their* hands dirty. The Pharisees and Essenes, each in their own way, represent this Withdrawal strategy: let us concern ourselves with keeping the Law of God inviolate, scrupulously adhering to the ritual commandments of the Lord, trusting that God will do his part and bring about his rule. We, meanwhile, will be holy.

Then there is the Terrorist strategy. At the heart of all terrorist activity, it appears, is despair. In Jesus' day, it was no different. The terrorists—in the Gospels they're called "Zealots"—despair because of the grinding poverty resulting from Roman taxation and the greed of the Palestinian upper classes; they despair at increasing landlessness, destitution, and skyrocketing debt for the peasant class; they despair that no one with the ability to make any difference cares about their plight. Those on the bottom of the socio-economic ladder knew that the "Peace of Rome" was no peace at all; "peace" was but a euphemism for an orderly oppression, for a grinding tyranny. They knew quite well that the peace of Rome was not the peace of God, and so they became terrorists. They decided they would do "whatever it takes" to bring down the empire.

No one mistakes the Sermon on the Mount for either the Super-Power strategy,[58] or the closely-related Accommodation strategy. Furthermore, the Sermon is clearly not a call for terrorist activity. In light of the available options, it appears that the Sermon must be a withdrawal from the realm of the social and political—or at best, the Sermon must not be related to the realm of the "real" social and political world.

A New Politics: Salt and Light

But this understanding of the Sermon fails to take into account another possibility: that Jesus envisioned and declared yet another alternative to the political strategies enumerated above. It is neither the way of the Super-Power, nor the way of Accommodation; neither the way of Withdrawal, nor the way of Terror. Jesus advocated a different way, the way of "salt and light." In ancient days, salt was multi-functional, serving as a preservative, a cleansing agent, or something that seasons bland food. In other words, salt was crucial to life.

And Jesus puts it this way: disciples are to the world as salt is to life. While it may be poor exegesis to narrow down the meaning of "salt" to any one of the above meanings, the "preservative" nature of salt provides a powerful metaphor;

since there was no refrigeration, in the absence of salt, meat rots, becomes a stinking mass of flesh, infested with maggots. And so we hear Jesus saying, "Unless you are salt, the world will rot. Unless you are salt and light, the world will continue hurtling toward death and destruction, reaping the natural results of its injustices and hatred and animosity and lust and warfare. Unless you embody the alternative of the good news of the Kingdom now present in your midst, the world will self-destruct. Unless you live according to your calling as a faithful witness to the new order among humankind, the world will continue falling headlong into the abyss."

When Puritan John Winthrop sailed from England in 1630, bound for the new colony of Massachusetts, he preached a sermon utilizing Matthew 5:14: "for we must consider that we shall be as a City upon a Hill, the eyes of all people are upon us." Ronald Reagan, the Republican who served as President from 1981-1988, liked Winthrop's metaphor so much that during his eight years of conservative presidential administrations, Reagan often referred to the U.S. as a "city on a hill." In his farewell radio address from the Oval Office, Reagan asserted that he had always sought to recover a vision of the U.S. as a "shining city set on a hill," offering a message of "freedom" to the world.

While the use of scriptural allusion often appeals to conservative Christians, many have failed to note that the sociological assumption supporting much presidential use of scriptural metaphors is fundamentally at odds with Jesus' sociological alternative. Jesus meant something very different when he told his disciples that they were salt, light, and like a city set upon a hill. Jesus was not referring to a classical, liberal, political order defended by a strong military. He was referring to the ways of the Kingdom of Heaven, which is an altogether different matter. With Reagan, for example, the United States sought to make the world safe for democracy by means of the threat of mutual nuclear destruction. Jesus instead declared that through *being* what God calls the world to be, through *offering* an alternative (not forcing change through sheer threat of annihilation), disciples simultaneously embody and proclaim the Good News.

Dietrich Bonhoeffer described the community of salt and light as "a visible community, their discipleship visible in action which lifts them out of the world." Gerhard Lohfink similarly says, "The radiant city on the hill is a symbol for the church as a *contrast-society*, which precisely as contrast-society transforms the world. If the church loses is contrast character, if its salt becomes flat and its light is gently extinguished . . . it loses its meaning."[59] In other words, if the church is to make any sustainable, real difference in the world, it will be by faithfulness to our calling as a people who walk in the way of Christ, not by being chaplains to a fallen order, by offering "spiritual advice" to those who would "run the world."

In Jesus' description of his followers as salt and light, he included an element of judgment upon the people of God if they fail to do what salt does: "become saltless" is more literally "foolish" or "insipid." "If you are not salty," Jesus seems to be saying, "you are good for nothing but to be cast out; if you refuse to be what you have been called to be, you are worthless."

THE OTHERNESS OF THE CHURCH

Jesus' way then, is to call followers, who as a community of believers embody that to which the world is called. The world was created *for* peace, was created *in* peace, and will return *to* peace. And so disciples are peaceable people in a world of violence. The world was not created for warfare, and warfare must be defeated; warfare cannot destroy warfare, only suffering love can destroy warfare. And so the people of the Kingdom love even enemies, in order to participate in God's destruction of hatred.

Sociologically, this is what is called a "sectarian" model. In E. Troeltsch's classic work, *The Social Teachings of the Christian Churches*, he did not intend a pejorative or derogatory judgment when he used the term "sectarian" to describe certain historical Christian movements. Instead, "sectarianism" meant an attitude that gives people a certain identity over against the larger world or larger culture of which they are a part. "Sectarianism" requires clear identifying markers that allow a clear definition of who is in and who is out, who is "faithful" and who is "not faithful."

In our tradition, "Sectarianism" has too often taken the shape of worship wars and issues of church polity. All those who agree with us (*me!*) on each issue we (*I!*) deem important, whether "they" accept the Lordship of Jesus or not, are "in" and all others are "out." This is what people typically mean by "sectarianism." "Conservatives" are depicted as those who are "sectarians," and "liberals" are depicted as those who are opposed to such "conservative sectarianism."

Arguments such as these—whether "conservative" or "liberal"—fail to get at the heart of the gospel and seldom address the kind of issues and assumptions undergirding the manner in which we have made the church irrelevant to the social and political questions of our world. Such arguments will continue to miss the point until we rediscover the *particular kind* of *sectarianism* (for there is, in one sense, no other word, sociologically, to use) that undergirds the

New Testament call to discipleship. There must exist a clear distinction between "the Church" and "the world." In the New Testament, the concrete "markers," if we wish to use that term, that distinguish the Church from the world are always rooted in the story and significance of the way of the cross and validated by the vindicating power of resurrection. The "world" constitutes those who refuse to accept the Lordship of Christ, who refuse to accept that the message of the cross is anything but foolishness; the "Church" constitutes precisely those who accept the word of the cross as God's (and therefore now the church's) means of bringing about reconciliation.

While sitting in the Birmingham jail after having been arrested for leading a non-violent protest of institutionalized racism, Martin Luther King, Jr. contrasted the churches of his day with the New Testament vision of the church:

There was a time when the church was very powerful. It was during that period when the early Christians rejoiced when they were deemed worthy to suffer for what they believed. In those days, the church was not merely a thermometer that recorded the ideas and principles of popular opinion; it was a thermostat that transformed the mores of society. Whenever the early Christians entered a town the power structure got disturbed and immediately sought to convict them for being "disturbers of the peace" and "outside agitators." But they went on with the conviction that they were "a colony of heaven," and had to obey God rather than man. They were small in number but big in commitment. They were too God-intoxicated to be "astronomically intimidated." They brought an end to such ancient evils as infanticide and gladiatorial contest.

Things are different now. The contemporary church is often a weak, ineffectual voice with an uncertain sound. It is so often the arch supporter of the status quo. Far from being disturbed by the presence of the church, the power structure of the average community is consoled by the church's silent and often vocal sanction of things as they are.

But the judgment of God is upon the church as never before. If the church of today does not recapture the sacrificial spirit of the early church, it will lose its authentic ring, forfeit the loyalty of millions, and be dismissed as an irrelevant social club with no meaning for the twentieth century.[60]

Put differently, King charged that the early church was salty, and the contemporary church saltless; the early church took discipleship seriously and thus bore witness to and embodied a powerful transforming alternative, while the contemporary church embodied and supported the fallen order, which desperately needed transformation.

A New Social Order

The "six antitheses" of Matthew 5:21-48 provide concrete examples of the alternative social and political order of the Kingdom. Not only shall we not murder, we shall take reconciliation seriously; we shall stop holding onto offenses between others and ourselves; if we have done wrong, we will go make it right (Matthew 5:21-26). Rather than treating women as objects (either through adultery, lust, or divorce), male citizens of the Kingdom are to honor spouses with commitments and vows that the ways of the world would call us to not take very seriously (Matthew 5:27-32). Rather than playing with words to get our way or further our agenda, we speak truthfully (Matthew 5:33-37).

Given the long debates over the meaning of the last two antitheses, that we "resist not evil" and that we "love our enemies," more extensive commentary is needed here, particularly since many have equated these with the

Withdrawal stance described above. More accurately put, many good-intentioned people have made Jesus' teaching here an admonition to be *passive* in the face of violence and injustice. So, the battered wife is told to "turn the other cheek," to say nothing to her husband but only bear the beatings. Or the boy bullied at school is told to "resist not evil," to say nothing, to do nothing, but just to "take it."

But the gospel is not a call to be passive in the face of evil; the love commanded by Jesus is *not* a sentimental, syrupy, sweet "love." This latter "love" could owe more to cowardice than to faithfulness. To advocate some sort of passive withdrawal from injustice, to advocate simple surrender and submission in the face of a tyrant, to be a doormat thereby making us a collaborator with despots and bullies—one must wonder if this is not simple spinelessness. Or one must wonder if it is not simple naïveté, a simple-minded trust in "being sweet," a simple faith that singing "Kum-Ba-Yah" will solve all the world's problems.

If we interpret Jesus' teaching in the Sermon as an admonition to passivity and "sweetness," we find all sorts of contradictions in the larger context of his life and ministry. Jesus never coddled the purveyors of hypocrisy, injustice, or oppression, but denounced such, calling them hypocrites, blind guides, and snakes (Matthew 23). In the presence of the ungodly agendas found in the temple court, Jesus turned over tables, drove out the animals with a whip, and demanded that those who were infesting his father's house be gone. Or when slapped at his trial, Jesus did not "turn the other cheek," but reprimanded the one who slapped him.

So what *do* these two "anti-theses" mean? Walter Wink's exegesis proves very helpful, suggesting that Jesus here advocates a "third way" between "fight or flight."[61] Rather than passivity on the one hand or retaliation on the other, Jesus teaches his disciples to seek a creative response to injustice that allows the perpetrator the grace to see his sins and extend the possibility that he might turn from them. For example, Jesus says, "if anyone strikes you on the *right* cheek. . . ." Given that the left hand was used only for unclean tasks, Jesus here envisions a backhanded slap with the right hand, a degrading insult of a superior to an inferior. The backhanded slap was symbolic of systematic oppression and was the means by which the one with power put the inferior "in his place." Whether master to slave, parent to child, man to woman, or Roman to Jew, the backhanded slap apparently left the one so insulted with only one of two options: retaliation (and subsequent retribution) or cowering submission, accepting the indignity without a word of objection.

But turning the other cheek is a third way, a notice given to the perpetrator of the insult. "Try again. Your first blow failed to achieve its intended effect. I deny you power to humiliate me. I am a human being just like you. Your status does not alter that fact. You cannot demean me."[62] Imagine the difficulty of trying to respond to a turned cheek: one would not use the left hand (even to gesture with the left hand at Qumran resulted in 10 days penance); and if you hit with a fist, you make the subordinate your peer; and with the left cheek now turned to you, it is logistically impossible to strike with another back-handed slap. If the point of a backhanding is institutionalized inequality, simply turning the other cheek disarms that power.

In our failure to take account of such context, "turn the other cheek" has become synonymous with passivity, but Jesus appears to be advocating something quite different—that we do *something* in response to injustice, but not the "something" modeled after the old-fashioned *lex talionis*, the "eye for an eye and a tooth for a tooth."

A court case in which one person is being sued provides another example. Luke's ordering helps us make more sense of this case. Luke's parallel reading records Jesus as saying that if someone seeks to take your "cloak," your "outer garment," then give the plaintiff your shirt, your "undergarment," as well (Luke 6:29). Among peasant people, clothing was sometimes their only form of property; and the outer garment was therefore used as collateral on loans (Exodus 22:25-27; Deuteronomy 24:10-13, 17). The law forbade keeping the cloak overnight, as the cloak was, among the very poor, used as something akin to a sleeping bag. In the example offered by Jesus, someone reduced to such poverty and oppressive debt is having his cloak taken away.

Jewish peasants lived in a culture of institutionalized economic oppression. "Heavy debt was...the direct consequence of Roman imperial policy."[63] "Trickle-down" economics certainly worked here: the heavy demands placed upon the wealthy had a harsh "trickle-down" effect upon the peasants. As the wealthy classes in Palestine wanted capital not easily liquidated and therefore not as easily taken for tax purposes by the empire, so the peasant landowners were continually pressured to give up their land. If the peasants were not willing to cede their rightful land claims, the wealthy could pry peasants off the land through the mounting pressure of debt and exorbitant interest rates, adding to the pressures of heavy taxation. Debtor court could be subsequently used to take what was wanted from the peasants. By Jesus' day, there were "large estates owned by absentee landlords, managed by stewards, and worked by tenant farmers, day laborers, and slaves. It is no accident that the first act of the

Jewish revolutionaries in 66 C.E. was to burn the Temple treasury, where the record of debts was kept."[64]

Jesus here envisions such a scene: a peasant being taken to court, his last possession—the cloak—being taken from him by a wealthy landowner. Jesus counsels the peasant to take off his undergarment, too! Hand it to the creditor! Just strip down right there in court, hand your garments to the greedy one, and walk out. Imagine the message such an action would send. Look at what you are doing! You're taking the very clothes off my back!

The point here is not *punitive*, but hopes for redemption. "Don't you see what you are doing—reducing an entire class of people to landlessness, abasement, and destitution?" As Wink puts it, "the Powers That Be literally stand on their dignity. Nothing depotentates them faster than deft lampooning." Jesus calls us to unmask the pretensions and cruelty of an unjust system in a way that allows change.

But such an interpretation appears at odds with Jesus' command, "do not resist him who is evil" (NASB), "do not resist an evildoer" (NRSV), or "do not resist an evil person" (NIV). Given this instruction, it seems inevitable that the subsequent instructions to "turn the other cheek" or "go the second mile" should be interpreted as an admonition to passivity in the face of injustice. While "resist" is clearly one possible meaning of *antistenai*, many fail to note that this word is very often used as a military term. Liddell-Scott defines the word thus: "set against esp. in battle, *withstand*." Wink reports that in the LXX, the word is used 44 of 71 times for militarily armed resistance; Josephus similarly uses the word 15 of his 17 usages; Philo 4 of 10.

In other words, against a backdrop of the many who desired to use arms against the great injustices of Roman oppression,

Jesus rejects lethal violence: "do not resist violently." Jesus rejects violent insurrection, rejects an agenda of vengeance-filled rebellion—just as Paul does in Romans 13. Though different language is used here, it appears Jesus means what is said numerous times elsewhere in the New Testament: Do not return evil for evil, and do not return like for like (see Romans 12:17, 21; 1 Peter 3:9; 1 Thessalonians 5:15). Regardless of one's interpretation of Matthew's understanding of the relation between Jesus and the Law, one thing is clear: the dynamic of the *lex talionis* is set aside. In response to the deep cultural faith that returning like for like is the means to preserve "justice," Jesus calls us to a different faith, a faith of God's will being more faithfully performed through the means of redemptive grace.[65]

In other words, Jesus gives us a third option to "fight or flight." Jesus admonishes those who are victims of injustice to find creative ways to deal with their oppression. Such a way extends both mercy and an opportunity for real change in the oppressor, and breaks the endless cycle of humiliation and counter-humiliation. Jesus teaches us to extend the same to others as has been extended to us: a grace that surprises, that neither gives you what you deserve ("an eye for an eye") nor allows you to presuppose your own self-righteousness and superiority as you dole out injustice upon others.[66]

This sense certainly fits the larger context of Jesus' life and ministry. Continually confronting evil, he consistently rejects the use of revenge and violence as the means to address injustice. Rather than returning blow for blow, rather than advocating a "justice" grounded in the *lex talionis*, rather than taking up the sword for the purposes of God's kingdom, Jesus advocates a different way: love of enemy. Love seeks the good of the enemy, the repentance of the enemy, and the transformation of the enemy so that the enemy might reflect the glorious image of God. Ultimately, love desires that the enemy come into the Kingdom of heaven.

The charge that Jesus' way is "not realistic" here meets its most difficult test. "You can't love those who don't love you. There are some people who don't respond to love, and they don't understand anything but violence." Those who would in this way set aside enemy love must account for the fact that Jesus deals with precisely this reality: "If you love those who love you, what reward do you have? Do not even the tax collectors do the same? And if you greet only your brothers and sisters, what more are you doing than others? Do not even the Gentiles do the same?" So, Jesus concludes, "Be perfect, therefore, as your heavenly Father is perfect." This command to "perfection" intends not some moral perfectionism, but a "perfect," complete, thorough love of enemies. We are called only to do what God has always done, loving those who do not love in return. By loving your enemies and praying for those who persecute you, you make yourself a child of God, bearing the marks of your heavenly Father, for "he makes his sun rise on the evil and on the good, and sends rain on the righteous and the unrighteous." God gives good gifts to people whether they deserve it or not; we should do the same, teaches Jesus. Grace thus becomes the operative social and political principle of the Kingdom.

HOW CHRISTIANS MAKE JESUS IRRELEVANT

Ironically, the mainstream of the Christian tradition tends to make Jesus *irrelevant* to recurring social, cultural, and political questions. The Sermon on the Mount, for example, is neatly set aside as applying only to "personal relations" not geo-politics; or "turning the other cheek" is trivialized and made to refer only to "personal insult" not a violent attack; or "love your enemy" is made to refer merely to the disciples' attitude of heart, not specific, concrete action in response to injustice. Such exegesis has a long history within Christendom. It is important to note that differences with regard to understanding the meaning of Jesus' teachings for Christian ethics are not rooted in mere, narrow exegetical questions. Instead, the different readings are grounded in much larger understandings of the meaning of "gospel" and "kingdom."

In the twentieth century, Foy E. Wallace towers above our history as a very significant player in undermining the social and political significance of Jesus' teaching. Under-girding Wallace's interpretation of the Sermon lies a crucial set of distinctions, which—ironically, given the insistence with which Wallace sought to set forth "New Testament Christianity"—owes much more to the likes of the Protestant Reformer Martin Luther than to the New Testament. Inasmuch as they have gone along with Wallace's program, twentieth-century Churches of Christ have betrayed their restoration principles, accepting long-standing commitments of Christendom projects that have replaced the authority of Jesus with some other authority.

To see the manner in which exegesis follows larger commitments and constructs, one must first consider the following sets of distinctions operative in Wallace's work:

Render to Caesar	Render to God
Civil relations	Religion
Civil government/the state	Church
Crime	Sin
Civil law	Morality
Secular	Spiritual

With such a construct in place, the Sermon on the Mount is neatly categorized as pertaining to the "spiritual," the "moral," and to "religion," but not to the "secular," "civil law," or to "civil relations." When Jesus proclaimed the "Kingdom of heaven," Wallace asserted that Jesus meant "the *reign* of heaven in the *hearts* of men." The purpose of Christ's kingdom is to establish

"The means of seeking and saving the lost humanity…. But the disciples of Christ—Christians—are not only citizens of a spiritual kingdom, we are all members of a civil community, and the principles of the *Sermon on the Mount* do not cancel our relationship to the organized society of which we are a part, nor exempt us from the civic obligations to it."[67]

In Wallace's purview, the gospel repeatedly takes on the nature of what we might call a "spiritual," as opposed to a social or political, message. So "blessed are the peacemakers" does not refer, he claims, to any who would actually mediate disputes or arguments, but to those who "preach peace," who preach the way one can be reconciled to God. Disciples are "salt of the earth" in providing some good for the earth. And what is the content of that good? "The new church would be a divinely founded society as an appointed means of rescuing the world from corruption." In other words, God has graciously provided a way to keep us from going to hell, and this is the fundamental point of the gospel: "the gospel reveals how God forgives sinners, how God makes man righteous, how God justifies sinful man," where man being "righteous" means humankind's justification before God. Thus, "Blessed are they which do hunger and thirst after righteousness" is a blessing pronounced upon those who long for "the justification that the gospel would bring to them in the pardon of sin." The gospel is a "system of justification" different from the Jews, imparting justification to sinners who demonstrate "obedience to the gospel which reveals it."[68]

Placing the Sermon on the Mount within its immediate context in Matthew and within its larger canonical context requires that we question Wallace's (and Luther's) interpretation of the gospel and the teaching of Jesus. As already indicated, Jesus declares the Kingdom as the rule of God "on earth, as it is in heaven." The Kingdom is not merely a "spiritual" reality, but the reality of God's rule finally being given its rightful place not only in the *hearts* of individual men and women, but in *every aspect* of human life, whether spiritual, social, cultural, or political. Taken in the larger canonical context of concern for God to bring about his justice, righteousness, and peace, Jesus announces the presence of precisely that reign. But it comes with a surprise — not in the way of defeat and destruction of one's enemies, nor the way of slaughter of one's opponents, nor in the way of the sword — but in the way of forgiveness, reconciliation, and love.

Wallace's construal of Jesus' teaching makes Jesus irrelevant to all such questions — Jesus can help you get to heaven, but he can't help you run the world. You'll need something else for that. The "responsibilities of citizenship in a civil society" require the use of an ethic other than the Sermon on the Mount. It appears that Wallace ultimately takes non-violence as irrelevant and impractical:

> The Christian who does not know how to deport himself in time of war, does not know how to deport himself in time of peace — the instructions are the same. The attitude that causes a Christian in time of war to appear as a freak specimen of humanity, and to be placed in a concentration camp, or in a federal prison, when the world is in distress and there is so much work to do, is no more practical in time of peace. A crisis merely brings it to light.[69]

There is something about Wallace's assumptions here, though, that is helpful. Wallace assumes that the way of Christ will not provide what is needed, to use my own words, to "run the world." It does, indeed, appear that Jesus' way will not provide us the means needed to "run the world." "Running the world" appears more akin to the way of the "Gentiles." Their way, according to Jesus, is to lord authority over others, to make things "turn out right," to "run the world." But "it is not so among you. For the Son of Man came not to be served, but to serve, and give his life as a ransom for many." Still, Wallace presumes that "running the world" is a Christian task, taking Romans 13 as his primary proof-text on this score.

From the biblical perspective, however, our task is not to "run the world," but to be salt and light, to bear witness to the new order that *God* is bringing into existence. The task of the Christian is first and foremost not to "make things turn out right," but to walk in faithful obedience to the way of Christ. This may lead to persecution, even death, but this was clearly anticipated by Jesus in his teaching to his followers. Yet the anticipation of persecution ought not to result in a betrayal of the way of Christ, for vindication and triumph of the Kingdom is guaranteed, and joy in the midst of suffering possible. "Blessed are you when people revile you and persecute you and utter all kinds of evil against you falsely on my account. Rejoice and be glad, for your reward is great in heaven, for in the same way they persecuted the prophets who were before you" (Matthew 5:11-12).

Justice & Racism

9 Justice, Racism & Churches of Christ

Doug Foster

Mr. A. M. Burton
Nashville, Tennessee

Dear Bro. Burton:

It has been brought to our attention that you have intentions of purchasing the St. Cecilia Academy property, for the purpose of using it as a school for Negroes.

...as elders of this congregation and residents of this community we view with concern the use of this property as a center for Negroes.

There are five white congregations of the Church of Christ in this vicinity. We feel that our congregation and also the others would be crippled in a short time because of the loss of much of our present membership and the hostility of the public to the Church of Christ if this Negro school were established.

We want you to understand that our opposition is not personal. We would oppose the present owners or any successors thereto if they should attempt the establishment of a Negro Project.

The Twelfth Avenue Church of Christ
By the Elders, May 8, 1953

Unfinished Reconciliation

Racial Attitudes in United States History

No issue in the history of the United States has permeated and shaped us and our institutions more profoundly than the matter of race.

In 1856, the U.S. Supreme Court stated in the Dred Scott decision that the words "all men are created equal" in the Declaration of Independence were never intended to include people of the African race, whether slave or free. They were regarded, the justices asserted, "as beings of an inferior order, and altogether unfit to associate with the white race, either in social or political relations; and so far inferior, that they had no rights which the white man was bound to respect."

Alexander Stevens, vice-president of the Confederate States of America, asserted that the protection of the institution of slavery was essential to regulate the inferior African race. In his two-volume work *The War Between the States* published soon after the war, Stephens reprinted a speech by Robert Toombs, the first Confederate Secretary of State. "The perfect equality of the superior race, and the legal subordination of the inferior, are the foundations on which we have erected our republican systems," Toombs insisted. And most Americans, north and south, agreed.

Even those who opposed slavery took for granted the inferiority of the black race. In the 1850s, states like Indiana, Iowa, and Illinois passed laws forbidding the immigration of any blacks, slave or free. Abolitionist leader Frederick Douglass, when on speaking tours with whites, was not allowed to eat with his white counterparts. Abraham Lincoln, in his debates with Stephen Douglas, repudiated any desire to bring social equality between the white and black races. Blacks, he said, were not fit to be voters, jurors, or office holders.

Reconstruction brought emancipation from slavery and a series of Constitutional amendments that gave the former slaves citizenship and equal rights. Reconstruction did not eradicate racism, however; it burned it deeper into the psyche of this nation. When Reconstruction ended, whites began the process of replacing slavery with a new system of separation and subordination. The crowning piece to this process was the landmark 1896 Plessy v. Ferguson Supreme Court decision. Louisiana law required trains operating in the state to provide separate cars for black and white passengers. Homer Plessy, a man with one-eighth black ancestry, was fined and imprisoned for attempting to ride on the white car. When the case reached the nation's highest court, it declared that no constitutional rights were violated by the Louisiana law. It was false to assume, they said, that "the enforced separation of the two races stamps the colored race with a badge of inferiority. If this be so, it is not by reason of anything found in the act, but solely because the colored race chooses to put that construction upon it."

A complex mesh of fear and hatred ruled the day in American race relations economically, politically, and religiously.

RACE AND RELIGION IN AMERICA

At first, many slave owners in America kept their servants from hearing the Gospel because they were afraid they might have to free them if they became Christians. Eventually, however, the churches insisted that masters teach Christianity to their slaves, assuring them that their slaves' spiritual state had nothing to do with their status as property.

Not until the Great Awakening of the 1730s and 1740s, however, did many slaves convert to Christianity. The emotional sermons of the revival preachers appealed to the disenfranchised slaves. By the beginning of the nineteenth century, tens of thousands of blacks had been converted, especially into those groups that appealed most to the "common people"—the Methodist and Baptist churches.

North or south, free or slave, when black Christians worshiped with their white sisters and brothers, they were constantly reminded in subtle, and not so subtle, ways of their inferior status. They were usually forced to sit in the back of the building or the balcony, and preachers constantly reminded slaves they must obey their masters if they wanted to go to heaven.

In the north, discrimination against black members of St. George's Methodist Church in Philadelphia led to the formation of the first black denomination—the African Methodist Episcopal Church—in 1787. In the south, free blacks in cities like Charleston, Mobile, and New Orleans formed independent churches, and masters often allowed slaves to hold their own meetings until the slave insurrection led by Methodist preacher Denmark Vesey in 1822. After that, Southern whites became increasingly nervous about any meetings of blacks without white supervision.

After the Civil War, the greatest growth of black churches in the south occurred when black members separated from their predominately white churches to form new black denominations. Southern Methodists allowed the formation of the Colored Methodist Episcopal Church in 1870. By 1874, Cumberland Presbyterians had organized the Colored Cumberland Presbyterian Church. And in 1886, most black Baptists in the United States came together to form the National Baptist Convention.

...I would like to suggest that you brethren at Lipscomb consider seriously the idea of putting an extension school at Nashville Christian Institute, and give the bright boys and girls an opportunity to get some college work.

When you send these Negro boys to Pepperdine for college work they are no longer any good for preaching in the South. We need to train Negro boys in the South. And the Lord knows the Negroes need some, at least a few college-trained men. When Keeble is gone what will they do?

J. Roy Vaughan
Gospel Advocate Company
December 13, 1962

The same thing happened in our own movement. Blacks, both slave and free, were members of churches in the Stone-Campbell Restoration Movement very early. In the 1851 report of the American and Foreign Anti-Slavery Society, "Campbellites" were recorded as owning 101,000 slaves. Many of those slaves learned the gospel and became members of local white congregations. As in other religious bodies, blacks were forced to sit separately from the white members and had a subordinate role in congregational matters. Within a few years of the end of the Civil War, however, black Christians in Restoration Movement churches formed their own separate congregations.

Significantly, the first major theological division in the Stone-Campbell Restoration Movement was happening at the same time. Many black congregations favored instrumental music and extra-congregational organizations. In 1878, black Christians established their own national organization—the

135

National Convention of the Churches of Christ (later changed to National Christian Missionary Convention). But as in the white churches, many blacks opposed such "innovations."

In Nashville, several black congregations had been established in the decades following the Civil War, including the Gay Street and Lea Avenue Christian Churches. Three leaders, Alexander Cleveland Campbell, George Phillip Bowser, and S. W. Womack, left Lea Avenue because of the innovations to form what would become the Jackson Street Church of Christ. All three had been influenced by the conservative teaching of David Lipscomb and became influential early leaders of black Churches of Christ. It was G. P. Bowser and a younger man, Marshall Keeble, however, who would become the most important leaders of the twentieth century.

G. P. Bowser received an education at Nashville's Walden University, a school for blacks operated by Methodists. There he studied scripture and literature, learned Greek and Hebrew as well as Latin, German, and French, and quickly rose in the African Methodist Episcopal Church. In 1897 he left the AME Church and was immersed at the Gay Street Christian Church, becoming a member at Lea Avenue.

Marshall Keeble was born near Murfreesboro, Tennessee in 1878. His family moved to Nashville when he was four, and it was here that he received his primary religious formation. He was baptized at the Lea Avenue Christian Church by its preacher Preston Taylor. However, under the influence of S. W. Womack, his future father-in-law, Keeble, along with Bowser, left Lea Avenue in opposition to the innovations.

Bowser and Keeble helped form and encourage other preachers like R. N. Hogan, Luke Miller, S. R. and A. L. Cassius, Levi Kennedy, G. P. Holt, and J. S. Winston. These and other leaders worked relentlessly and selflessly in the midst of a blatantly racist society in the first half of the twentieth century. They baptized tens of thousands from Florida to Michigan to California. In 1903, G. P. Bowser began a paper he named the *Christian Echo*—one of the longest-running religious publications in America.

The remarkable work of such preachers created the black Churches of Christ that today number over 1200 congregations with almost 170,000 members. Yet segregation was and is virtually absolute. Whites in Churches of Christ were firmly in the grips of the prevailing American mindset. A few voices ran counter to the worst sentiments. Early in the century, David Lipscomb labeled segregation and race prejudice a sin and an outrage that should not be tolerated and insisted churches that condoned such a spirit had forfeited their claims to be a church of God.

But even Lipscomb was not immune from the deeply ingrained notions of black inferiority. Paternalism was the most common relationship between black and white Churches of Christ in the years before the Civil Rights Movement. White benefactors supported preachers like Keeble, who clearly "knew their place," and white churches made sure that their black brothers and sisters had *separate* places to meet. On the other hand, blacks like Bowser who took a more militant stance against racial discrimination often found it difficult to survive financially. A. B. Lipscomb, a nephew of David, epitomized the paternalistic attitudes in a 1931 *Gospel Advocate* article describing the success of Marshall Keeble in an evangelistic effort among blacks in Valdosta, Georgia.

"The work among the colored people here was sponsored and financed by the white disciples. We have never made a better investment for the Lord nor any which brought such quick and happy results. . . . This means that we now have better farm hands, better porters, better cooks, better housemaids than ever before."

There was an even uglier side of racism in Churches of Christ. Foy E. Wallace, Jr., in the March 1941 *Bible Banner*, for example, berated whites who attended Negro meetings and praised the black preachers for their work. He concluded by saying that "if any of the white brethren get worked up over what I have said, and want to accuse me of being jealous of the negro preachers, I will just tell them now that I don't even want to hold a meeting for any bunch of brethren who think that any negro is a better preacher than I am!"

The racist attitudes seen in the churches were also reflected in our schools. We bought so thoroughly and blindly into ungodly American cultural standards that it was simply unthinkable that blacks would be allowed to attend our Christian colleges. The few attempts to create schools for blacks in the Movement were mostly left to struggle and die from lack of support. Two schools, however, Nashville Christian Institute (1940-1967) and Southwestern Christian College, begun in 1950, would become key institutions in the formation of an identity for the black Churches of Christ.

CHURCHES OF CHRIST AND THE CIVIL RIGHTS MOVEMENT

It is my great hope and desire that the doors of all our congregations and of all our schools, from the least to the greatest, will be thrown open to all men everywhere (as they should be) regardless of race and color. So soon as we learn that God has of one blood made all nations of men and expects us to have no respect of persons (James 2:1) even as he does (Romans 2:11), that soon—and no sooner—will we have a right to say we are a restoration of New Testament Christianity with respect to this question. As long as we rationalize our white-man's misbehavior in excluding some of our brethren from our society (hence from our fellowship) because of their race, color or any other inconsequential over which they have no possible control—that long we may call ourselves Christians and churches of Christ, but our calling us that won't make it so.

Ira Y. Rice, Jr.
June 30, 1964

In a stunning 1954 ruling, the U.S. Supreme Court reversed the Plessy v. Ferguson decision of 1896. On May 17, the Court unanimously ruled in Brown v. Board of Education that the "separate but equal" doctrine was unconstitutional. In the words of Chief Justice Earl Warren, "segregated schools are not equal and cannot be made equal, and hence [black children] are deprived of the equal protection of the laws." This ruling and the events of the next few years began the Civil Rights Movement that would ironically drive black and white Churches of Christ even farther apart.

Many older members of black Churches of Christ eyed Martin Luther King, Jr. and the Civil Rights Movement with suspicion. These people were not "members of the church" after all. Yet, it was a black lawyer trained at Keeble's Nashville Christian Institute who played a significant role in the fight for equality in American society. Fred Gray grew up in the Holt Street Church of Christ in Montgomery, Alabama. Between 1944 and 1947, he accompanied Keeble in his travels across the country. After overcoming great obstacles to become a lawyer, he was thrust into the early events of the Civil Rights Movement. Gray defended Rosa Parks and Martin Luther King, Jr. in the days of the Montgomery Bus Boycott and prosecuted Civil Rights desegregation cases throughout the south. This made many black Christians nervous about Gray. Gray reports in his autobiographical work, *Bus Ride to Justice*, that when a preacher said to Keeble, "Fred Gray is smart. He is involved in the Civil Rights Movement," Keeble replied, "He's too smart."

As was the case throughout American Christianity, white Churches of Christ in the South and in other parts of the country resisted the implications of Civil Rights legislation for our churches and schools. While there were militant segregationists in white congregations—even members of the Ku Klux Klan—the majority took the gentler approach of gradualism. "We just need to go slow," they insisted. "Let's not upset those who have deep-seated prejudices against blacks, but work toward a gradual change in the situation." In effect, this appeal to gradualism was actually a strategy to maintain segregation indefinitely.

The years 1967 and 1968 were pivotal in the history of relations between black and white Churches of Christ. Four events took place that would effectively end the paternalism of the past and seal the pattern of virtually total separation that continues to this day. These events were not *meant* to seal the division—just the opposite. Nevertheless, the result was the final creation of two separate churches divided by race.

The first was the abrupt closing of Nashville Christian Institute in 1967. The Board of the school had started as an all black group, but within a few years, it was evenly divided between blacks and whites. Many of the whites also served on the Board of David Lipscomb College. The property was sold for over $225,000, and the proceeds given to Lipscomb to provide scholarships for black students. The black Christians who had sacrificed for years to keep the school going and who saw it as central to the identity of the black church were shocked. With the aid of Fred Gray, some of the alumni attempted to sue David Lipscomb College, hoping to use the funds for Southwestern Christian College — the only remaining black school in Churches of Christ. They were unsuccessful, and for many black Christians this event remains a defining moment in their relation to white Churches of Christ.

For several years during the time I was on the faculty at Lipscomb in the 1980's, I served on the Teacher Education Committee. Part of the money from the sale of Nashville Christian Institute was designated to go to black members of Churches of Christ who were going to be teachers. Every year we confronted what at the time was to me a puzzling apathy by black preachers and congregational leaders toward our appeals to encourage their young people to attend Lipscomb. In conversations with some of those leaders in the "One-in-Christ" meetings sponsored by ACU over the past two years, I have come to understand it better. "For all those years you refused to allow any of us to attend your school, then you took by force and against our will one of the only rallying points we had, let it be swallowed up in your multi-million dollar operation and then you say to us, 'You can come over here and be like us now. We still don't particularly value your culture and history and the way you live, and act, and worship, but you can come over here with us, as long as you just do like we do.' Can you understand the resentment expressed at this act?"

The second event was the race relations workshop hosted on March 4-8, 1968, by the Schrader Lane Church of Christ in Nashville. Eleven speakers addressed the integrated audience and pulled no punches. Schrader Lane's preacher, David Jones, opened the series by attacking blacks in their acquiescence to the paternalism of the white churches. Another black minister, James Dennis, Sr., frankly stated, "the Negro . . . feels suspicion of the white man, for he has not learned to trust his word. He feels antagonistic because he is not wanted." White businessman Bud Stumbaugh accused whites of figuratively amputating the legs of black people, then criticizing them for being crippled. Walter Burch, a white businessman from New York, contended that the "shameful specter of discrimination and racial injustice implicitly sanctioned by our brotherhood . . . patently nullifies the claim of Churches of Christ to have restored New Testament Christianity."

Many in the Nashville white churches boycotted the meeting. It was, in the words of organizers, "only a small beginning." How things developed subsequently would be the crucial test of its true significance.

The third event was the publication of the July 1968 issue of *Twentieth Century Christian*. A special issue on "Christ and Race Relations," co-edited by Walter Burch (white) and Eugene Lawton (black), it was a bold move for this widely circulated magazine. In a private letter written in 1979, Walter Burch characterized the issue's publication as "a miracle somewhat akin to the parting of the Red Sea." The magazine's printer resisted the effort right down until press time. The issue carried frank and confrontational articles attacking racism in Churches of Christ. Jennings Davis contended that "It is Time to Confess Our Sins." John Allen Chalk wrote of "Total Equality in Christ" and Roosevelt Wells of "The Contradiction of Racist Christianity." Again, the effort was a sign of hope. But many in Churches of Christ seemed to think otherwise. According to one report, the magazine lost half its subscribers because of the issue.

The final event was the Atlanta Conference on Race

Relations held June 25-26, 1968, called by black leaders Eugene Lawton and Roosevelt Wells and white leader Jimmy Allen. Forty-seven men attended, including ministers, college presidents, and journal editors. At the end of the meeting, a statement was produced acknowledging the sin of racial prejudice in Churches of Christ and church-related institutions and businesses. It set out specific guidelines to remedy the evil in congregations, schools, the Herald of Truth, publishing houses, and Christian-owned businesses. Twelve of the forty-seven present refused or otherwise failed to sign.

The events of these two years revealed deep division in the midst of high expectations. A beginning had been made in admitting the evil of segregation and racism. But the potential was simply not realized. Racism and segregation remained the norm, and black church leaders who had cautiously participated in the efforts, saw that their white sisters and brother were, for the most part, not interested in change.

The end of paternalism and the final radical separation of black and white Churches of Christ was symbolized by a 1968 *Christian Chronicle* article written by Jack Evans. He referred to the court action against Lipscomb in the Nashville Christian Institute case and declared it "was one of the first signs that many of the 100,000 who make up a negro brotherhood, separated from the white brotherhood by scars far deeper than the railroad tracks in Terrell, Texas, are ready to exchange servility and dependence for independence and, if need be, estrangement." The die was cast for another generation, and the two fellowships went their separate ways. The hurts, the suspicions, and the anger remained because the sin remained. And for the most part, it still remains.

RACE AND LIPSCOMB UNIVERSITY

Like most of our colleges in Churches of Christ, Lipscomb did not allow blacks to attend for the majority of its history. In the spring quarter of 1965, James William Fitzgerald, 37, enrolled and took classes at Lipscomb—the first black student to do so after it was quietly decided that the school could no longer keep blacks from entering. The previous year, the most important piece of civil rights legislation since Reconstruction had been signed by President Johnson, outlawing discrimination based on race, color, religion, or national origin in public establishments. The 1964 act was sweeping in that it used the federal government's power to regulate interstate commerce to outlaw discrimination in private business. Segregation, whether in restaurants, public accommodations, or public colleges, was officially outlawed. True, as a private religious school, Lipscomb could have "held out," as Bob Jones University and a few others did. But there was a kicker: no institution, public or private, could receive federal aid and remain discriminatory.

A widespread story had long-time Lipscomb president Athens Clay Pullias making the statement that if blacks tried to come on the Lipscomb campus, he would personally meet them at the entrance with a baseball bat and make sure they didn't. Whether or not the story is true, the college certainly did not welcome blacks. Opening the doors to black students didn't happen when it did primarily because people suddenly realized the utter sinfulness of such arrogance and respect of persons. It happened when it did, ultimately, because if Lipscomb had continued to exclude blacks, they would have lost massive federal funds—funds already being secured for projects like the science building.

If Lipscomb's board was anything like ACU's Board at that time, there were a few who saw the evil of segregation and discrimination and who worked to move the school toward a Christian stance on race. Someone ought to name and honor them. There were likely some old-time segregationists as well, with an even larger number in the middle, wary of doing anything that would alienate their still all-too-white constituency. And the student body undoubtedly reflected the same attitudes. The overall atmosphere was not conducive to encouraging blacks to attend, though they were now allowed to do so.

It's no surprise, then, that few blacks actually enrolled at Lipscomb in the years after the initial integration. It was still a "white" school. Black culture was not honored. Black students found it hard to fit in. There was little sensitivity to students having to deal with a setting that largely depreciated their uniqueness or ignored them. Then, when Nashville Christian Institute was abruptly closed in 1967 over the protests of black leaders and its assets turned over to the all-white Lipscomb administration, the anger and alienation increased and to this day remains intense for many of our sisters and brothers of color.

"But things are different now. All this was thirty plus years ago. Things are much better now. We have moved beyond race hatred and, while things may not be perfect, the problems are pretty much solved and we are moving on." I don't think so!

In one sense, it is true that we can see progress in the matter of race relations. The kind of overt separation and subordination of the black race instituted by white supremacists after the Civil War has been outlawed. No longer can whites literally get away with murder because their victim was black. No longer can people be excluded from restaurants, hotels, theaters, and colleges—even private Christian colleges—because of the color of their skin. In many ways, things are better than they used to be, at least at first glance.

But something is still badly wrong. In the recent Oxford University Press publication *Divided by Faith*, authors Emerson and Smith argue that "by 1964, as the formally segregated public sphere receded, an informally segregated private sphere began to rise in its place." Blacks and whites ironically have come to know less and less about each other in this new situation. Younger generations were less overtly racist than their parents were, but there was in many ways an increase in the distance between the races. "Racialization," as they call it, "although changed in its form, remained ever present."

This is precisely what happened to our churches in the 1960s, as Black Churches of Christ had been in a paternalistic relationship to white churches since the beginning of the century. But in the decade of the 60s a completely separate and independent black Church of Christ was organized around its informal institutions: the *Christian Echo*, the National Lectureship, the Annual National Youth Conference, and Southwestern Christian College. Overall, blacks and whites in our churches know less about each other at the beginning of the 21st century than in previous times.

We whites thought that integration of our churches and schools would take care of the problems. The truth is that mere integration neither resolves the problem nor absolves the sin. In fact, mere integration creates new problems that are perhaps more subtle, insidious, and destructive than those it was meant to solve. Mere integration erodes the strengths of the minority culture. It says in effect, "now we'll let you come over and be like us. But don't expect us to change—after all, we're already at the top. If you want to do well, you'll act and think like us."

Racialization means division along the lines of race. There is no question that this nation and the Churches of Christ are just that—divided by race. The 1998 Congregation Studies Project revealed that ninety percent of American congregations are made up of at least 90% of people of the same race. Why is this so? Something is not right. It is easy to say that people of the different races simply prefer to be with others of their own race. Blacks prefer to worship with other blacks, whites with other whites. Fine—but why is that so? Well, we have different cultural values, different ways of expression, different preferences in style. Okay, but why does that mean that we must be segregated? Why does that mean that Christians of different races must be separate rather than together in the most intimate and unity-producing actions Christians perform?

Emerson and Smith reported that:

When white evangelicals spoke of integrating congregations, they meant that their specific congregation ought to be open to all people. They did not mean that they should consider going to a mixed or nonwhite congregation. No one spoke about this possibility. Further, no one spoke of the need for the congregation to adapt or diversify the way it does things to become racially mixed. This means that it must be other people, not them, who would have to make the change. In this light, although they may support congregational integration, it is difficult to conceive of it actually happening on any large scale as a result of that support.

Those who did not support the mixed race congregations idea were fairly pragmatic in their reasons. Comfort and enjoyment were common themes. In the words of one Christian Reformed man, "I think the whole concept of blacks and whites worshipping together is great, but how can you do that when you feel so uncomfortable?"

In an October 2, 2000 article in *Christianity Today* dealing with the issue of race in American churches, theologian J. I. Packer stated a truth of the gospel that many of us are only beginning to realize. "Being in the kingdom of God has to do with self-denial and cross-bearing and living a life in which instability and problems and relational headaches of one sort or another are par for the course. This isn't comfort zone stuff."

Something is not right. Emerson and Smith point out that for the most part conservative Christians in this country have taken the position that the best approach to racial reconciliation is individual reconciliation, that the key to ending racial division is for individuals of different races to develop strong personal relationships with people of the other race and repent of individual prejudice. There is no question that this is key to the process—this is godly and biblical and necessary. But we have not been very keen on targeting the institutions, the social systems that actually do the discriminating, that actually impose injustice and inequality. We have avoided the idea that institutions—even good ones like Lipscomb and Abilene Christian Universities—can be guilty of and need to repent of sin.

Quoting a black minister in Los Angeles, Emerson and Smith assert that "calling sinners to repentance means also calling societies and structures to repentance.... The gospel at once works with the individual and the individual's society; to change one, we of necessity must change the other."

The conviction of this truth is in part behind the recent racial reconciliation efforts made by Lipscomb and ACU. Dr. Steve Flatt, Lipscomb's President since 1998, in a chapel address on September 7 that year, stated that Lipscomb was at one time guilty of overt racism. "Sadly, instead of leading the way, otherwise devout white Christians were blinded by culture and Satan's lie that white and black students should not be educated in the same setting.... I hate that. I deeply regret that, and as president, I now apologize for that." That same year Lipscomb established an office of Multicultural Affairs to help make Lipscomb a place where cultural and ethnic diversity was valued.

Because of a sense of frustration and of the wrongness of the *de facto* racialization of our churches, ACU's President, Dr. Royce Money, began contacting leaders in black Churches of Christ to discuss what might be done to begin to heal the division that has existed so strongly since the 1960s. A meeting was called for October 1999 that drew twenty-five black and ten white leaders to the ACU campus. At times, the meeting was tense. Several of the men in attendance had been denied admission to ACU, Harding, or Lipscomb before integration. Several expressed strong hostility over the memory of the closing of Nashville Christian Institute. No subject was banned from the conversation.

At the end of the two days, after kneeling together in small groups to pray for one another, Royce Money and ACU Board chair Don Crisp asked the forgiveness of those present for ACU's past sins of discrimination. They then offered to attend the Southwestern Christian College Lectures the next month—one of the largest annual gatherings of black members of Churches of Christ—and make a formal, public acknowledgment of the same. On November 22, 1999, Money said the following:

Abilene Christian University has been a Christian institution of higher education for more than 90 years. Its doors were not open to African-American students for well over half that time. We are here today to confess the sins of racism and discrimination and to

149

issue a formal apology to all of you, to express regret and to ask forgiveness.

We understand from the Lord that part of repentance involves the resolve to go in a different direction from the past. But before we focus on the future, we need to confess the sins of racism and discrimination of the past against our African-American brothers and sisters. We are truly sorry.

This kind of repentance must happen in many other of our institutions that are guilty of racism before true racial reconciliation can begin. There are plenty of reasons not to do it.

1. *"None of us were in charge when the discriminatory policies were in place.* We had nothing to do with all that. How can you repent of something you didn't do?" That's where the exclusive focus on individual reconciliation becomes the killer. We are part of an institution that sinned. It has never publicly asked forgiveness of that sin from the people against whom it sinned. The wounds of that racial sin run deep. Are we going to say as the Supreme Court did in 1896, that it's the blacks' problem, not ours? If we do, something is deeply wrong. Repentance is the right thing to do.

2. *"We just need to forget it and move ahead.* If we keep dwelling on past mistakes, it just reopens old wounds." You can't move ahead and leave the mistakes of the past until you have admitted them, repented of them, and asked forgiveness for them. It's still the right thing to do.

3. *"If you're going to apologize to blacks, why not apologize to native Americans, and the Chinese, and every other group that you've ever treated badly."* This may be true. But it makes no sense to say

that you shouldn't right one wrong because you might have others to deal with. It's still the right thing to do.

4. *"You're just doing it for political and economic reasons—you just want to tap the market for more black students to increase your revenue."* Only God can know the heart, and our motivations are always mixed. If that were the motivation, then a statement of repentance would be manipulative and corrosive to those who make it. The fruit will eventually be seen. The fruit that has come from the repentance of Lipscomb and ACU is beginning to come in, and it looks pretty good so far. But God uses even insincere people to change the hearts and minds of the sincere—the gospel itself was preached from bad motives at times. It's still the right thing to do.

Race hatred and racial discrimination and segregation is not a mistake; it is sin. It is sin now, and it was sin then. If that sin was not recognized in times past by members of Churches of Christ in America, then God's grace will have to cover it. But *we* can see it, I pray. And we can do something about it.

As hard as it is to admit, the church will always be flawed and sinful because human beings are flawed and sinful. Only through repentance and the mercy of Christ can such sins be forgiven and reconciliation be completed. We must pray for wisdom and spiritual discernment to see the sins to which we are NOW blinded so that they do not become a part of our identity. The actions now being taken toward reconciliation between black and white Churches of Christ are the result of the fruit of the Spirit. May God continue this beginning work among us to His glory!

10 A Journey to Freedom

Kenneth R. Greene

I was born in a small community called Belleview located in the city of Winston-Salem, N.C. My parents were born and reared there also. In Belleview, a small community with approximately eight hundred Whites and five hundred African-Americans, two important realities shaped my consciousness: the African-American church experience and the socio-political significance of the White people.

The African-American church introduced me to the essence of life as expressed in the rhythm and feelings of African-American people in Belleview. In the African-American church, I encountered the presence of the divine Spirit, and my soul was moved and filled with an aspiration for freedom. Through prayer, song, and sermon, God made frequent visits to the African-American community in Belleview and reassured the people of his concern for their well-being and his will to bring them safely home.

Home was often identified with heaven — that otherworldly reality beyond the reach of the dreadful limitations of this world. It was that place on the other side of Jordan, down by the riverside, where the streets are gold and the gates are pearly. Home was that eschatological reality where the oppressed world lay down that heavy load, singing and shouting because there would be nobody there to turn him or her out. Every Sunday, the brothers and sisters of the African-American church experienced a foretaste of their home in glory. God's Spirit visited their worship, and they responded with thankfulness, humility, and joyful singing.

"Soon I will be done with the troubles of this world.
Soon I will be done with the trouble of this world.
Going home to live with God."

The African-American church taught me how to deal with the contradictions of life and provided a way to create meaning in a community. This perspective on life is often called the "art of survival"; but in the African-American church, we call it the grace of God. It is called "survival" because it is a way of remaining physically alive in a situation of oppression without losing one's dignity. We call it grace because we know it to be an unearned gift from him who is the giver of every good and perfect gift. This is what African-American people mean when they sing, "We've come this far by faith, leaning on the Lord, trusting in His holy Word."

Unfortunately, the African-American church experience was not my only experience in Belleview. The presence of eight hundred Whites made me realize, at an early age, that African-American existence cannot, indeed must not, be taken for granted. White people did everything within their power to define African-American reality, to tell us who we were—and their definition, of course, extended no further than their social, political, and economic interests. They tried to make us believe that God created African-American people to be White people's servants. We African-Americans, therefore, were expected to enjoy plowing their fields, picking their cotton, cleaning their houses, mowing their lawns, and working in their tobacco fields. When we showed signs of displeasure with our so-called elected and inferior status, they called us uppity niggers and quickly attempted to put us in our place.

To be in one's place, defined by White society, was a terrible reality for African-Americans in Belleview. It meant being beaten by the town cop and spending an inordinate length of time in a stinking jail. It meant attending "separate but equal" schools, going to the balcony when attending a movie, and drinking water from a "colored" fountain. It meant refusing to retaliate when called a "nigger" — unless you were prepared to leave town at the precise moment of your rebellion. You had no name except your first or "boy"; and if you were past the age of sixty-five, you might attain the dubious honor of being called "uncle" or "auntie." Those are the two important realities that shaped my consciousness: the African-American church experience and the socio-political significance of White people.

THE STRESS OF HUMAN SERVITUDE

African-Americans had to feel their way along the course of American slavery, enduring the stress of human servitude, while still affirming their humanity. How could this be? How was it possible for African-American people to keep their humanity together in the midst of servitude, affirming that the God of Jesus was at work in the world, liberating them from bondage? The record shows clearly that African-American slaves believed that, just as God had delivered Moses and the Israelites from Egyptian bondage, he also would deliver African-Americans from American slavery. And they expressed theological truth in song:

> Oh Mary, don't you weep, don't you moan,
> Oh Mary, don't you weep, don't you moan,
> Pharaoh's army got drowned,
> Oh, Mary, don't you weep.

That truth did not come from White preachers; it came from a liberating encounter with the One who is the Author of African-Americans' faith and existence. What is the source and meaning of freedom expressed in this spiritual?

> Oh freedom! Oh freedom!
> Oh freedom! I love thee!
> And before I'll be a slave,
> I'll be buried in my grave
> And go home to my Lord and be free.

Here freedom is obviously a structure of, and a movement in, historical existence. It is African-American slaves accepting the risk and burden of self-affirmation, of liberation in history. That is the meaning of the phrase, "and before I'll be a slave, I'll be buried in my grave." Without negating history, the last line of this spiritual places freedom beyond the historical context, "and go home to my Lord and be free." In this context, freedom is eschatological. It is the anticipation of freedom, a vision of a new heaven and a new earth. That affirmation enabled African-Americans to meet "the man" on Monday morning and to deal with his dehumanizing presence the remainder of the week, knowing that White folks could not destroy their humanity.

From the Bible handed to African-Americans by their

oppressors, the African-Americans hewed out for themselves a Christian theology of freedom—an ingenious feat. So, there moved in that small community of Belleview a mood that raced like a tidal wave, relentlessly lashing against the shores of bondage until the quest for freedom would be secured. African-Americans were intent on being free in Jesus Christ. From their crude knowledge of the gospel of Jesus Christ emerged a message of freedom for African-Americans that their oppressors failed to disclose. African-Americans vowed never to rest until that freedom was realized.

EVASIVE FREEDOM

The era of Dr. Martin Luther King, Jr. brought about great strides toward freedom. African-Americans now seem to be enjoying a liberty that is unprecedented in all the years of their sojourn in this country. The spirit of freedom pervades the land as a result of the Civil Rights era. Women are free. Gay people are free. Everyone is free.

But is this freedom as real as it appears? This is a prevailing question of our day. Strong suspicions surface that the answer to the question is less than affirmative. Examples of bondage and oppression in our society are almost too numerous to mention; but mention some we must.

The U.S. African-American infant mortality rate in 2000 placed 28th worldwide, behind such nations as Cuba and Bulgaria and equal to Costa Rica and Poland. African-American infant mortality rates are higher in Memphis, the District of Columbia, Indianapolis, and Boston than in Jamaica.

The nation's overall unemployment rate is 5.9 percent. Among African-Americans, it is 12.1 percent and among Hispanics, it is 9.1 percent. The national teenage unemployment rate is 16.8 percent, nearly three times the national average for all groups. The unemployment rate for African-American teens stands at 34.3 percent. Between 1977 and 2000, the percentage of 18- to 24-year-old white high school graduates entering college increased from 51 to 56 percent. The percentage of African-American college-bound seniors declined from 50 to 36.5 percent, and the percentage of Hispanics declined from 51 to 44.4 percent.

And if that's not enough, there is a move to make more certain, though subtle, the bondage of African-Americans. The Supreme Court ruling in the Allen Bakke case indicates erosion in the sentiment that, inasmuch as America has done much to keep African-Americans down, America must now do much to raise them up. The stride of African-Americans toward freedom has been reduced to a crawl by soaring inflation and towering unemployment.

It is not enough just to recognize the various bondages that African-Americans, Browns, and the poor are confronting in this country. We must rally to do something about them. It's not enough just to analyze our condition, because we can become victims of paralysis by analysis. The examples of people in bondage in America could go on and on—Native Americans, Mexican Americans. What is the answer to this question of bondage in American society?

Freedom in America is not as free as it appears. Even those who seem to be free are ensnared by a peculiar kind of bondage: bondage of narcissism, money, quest for power, fear of sickness, and fear of death.

Freedom is evasive; it is an illusion. There still stands before the children of bondage the pressing assignment to claim their freedom.

A Journey to Freedom

Determined to Be Free in Jesus Christ

Freedom for African-Americans in this country did not
come by fiat ("Let it be done."), i.e., from the Emancipation
Proclamation of Abraham Lincoln. It came from African-
Americans' determination to be free in Jesus Christ, from their
crude knowledge of the gospel of Jesus Christ, from which
emerged a message of freedom for African-Americans that
their oppressors failed to disclose. African-Americans vowed
never to rest until that freedom was realized.

Freedom meant African-American men marrying the
women they loved and establishing families. It meant securing
land and beginning a farm. It meant earning a living for
oneself and one's family by industry and ingenuity. It meant
becoming a part of the federal and state political apparatus
in order to participate in the process of regulating the lives
of African-Americans and assuring freedom's continuance.
It meant the establishment of churches, associations,
conventions, and organizations to perpetuate the religious
unity of the people. It meant the establishment of schools for
the religious and secular education of African-Americans. It
meant the establishment of businesses, insurance companies,
banks, and publishing houses to assure the economic security
of African-Americans. It meant a return to the high ethics and
morals known to African-Americans before they were forcibly
made slaves and participants in a perverted and promiscuous
culture.

All of this grows out of a clear vision and determination
to be free in Christ Jesus. Through his life, we are living.
Through his breath, we are breathing. Through his teaching,
we are taught. Through his comfort, we are comforted. His
hand holds us. Upon his shoulder we can lean. Through our

faith, we cannot fail. Through his power, we shall prevail. Through his death, we shall live again.

Yet, at the beginning of the 20th century, something happened to African-Americans in their determination to be truly free. The sin of shrinking back emerged in the fiber of their personality, blurred their vision, and prevented them more and more from keeping their eyes on the bright and morning star of freedom in Jesus Christ as expressed in Hebrews 10:19-39. And today, African-Americans have committed the sin of shrinking back, born of the fickleness they encountered at the turn of the century. African-Americans have turned to a varied assortment of religions that offer no true freedom, leaving the soul in spiritual bondage. They failed to follow the Christian faith that provided the Spirit and power to move them from oppression to freedom. They made a tremendous beginning in that direction, but they fell to the fatal sin of shrinking back.

In the first quarter of the 20th century, James Weldon Johnson, the son of an African-American preacher of the Christian gospel, wrote the song, "Lift Every Voice and Sing," in an attempt to check this great reversal. One verse in particular called African-American people to remain faithful to the God who brought them through slavery:

God of our weary years, God of our silent tears,
Thou who hast brought us thus far on the way
Thou who hast by thy might, led us into the light
Keep us forever in the path we pray.
Lest our feet stray from the place, our God,
   where we met Thee.
Lest our Heart, drunk with the vine of the world,
   forget Thee.
Shadowed beneath Thy hand, may we forever stand,
True to our God, true to our native land.

Yet the great shrinking back continues. The Martin Luther King, Jr. era of Civil Rights came, and once again the Christian faith proved to be the religion to provide the Spirit and power to end segregation and de-humanization for African-Americans. But though Dr. King made a breakthrough to secure freedom in America for African-Americans, after his assassination, African-Americans failed to follow through by taking that same Christian gospel that was a part of King's arsenal to continue their battle for freedom. In the next three chapters, we will look at three battlefronts for freedom: the African-American family, African-American churches, and White institutions.

11 What African-American Families Need to Hear

Kenneth R. Greene

I contend that if there is going to be any hope for the oppressed African-American family, there first must be a renewed vision and commitment to the resurrected Christ, to him who "came to proclaim release to the captives and recovering the sight to the blind, to set at liberty those who are oppressed" (Luke 4:18f.).

ABANDONMENT OF MORALS

Not only have African-Americans abandoned the Christian faith, but we are in bondage as well because we have abandoned morality. When a people's religious faith is shattered and shaken into confusion, it loses sight of the moral imperatives in life. This happened to African-Americans at the turn of the twentieth century, when an increase in aberrant religious expressions arose. Concomitant with this was a decrease in morality among people.

Native African people were highly moral before their introduction into American slavery. They knew nothing of untruthfulness, drunkenness, sexual immorality, or perversity. Immorality among African-Americans is a child of American slavery.

163

Yet, African-Americans never allowed such immorality
to deter their quest for freedom, a freedom they had been
assured was theirs by the gospel of Jesus Christ. As they broke
their chains of human bondage, simultaneously they flung
from themselves the yoke of immorality. Freedom for African-
Americans also meant marriages and moral decency.

After emancipation, and through much of the 20th
century, African-Americans overcame racism, segregation,
and Jim Crow laws, striving to preserve their families. Herbert
Gutman, in *The Black Family in Slavery and Freedom*, found that
in the early 1900's, African-Americans' marriages endured
at about the same rate as those of Whites of similar socio-
economic levels. He also noted that in North and the South,
"the typical Afro-American family was lower-class in status and
headed by two parents." Even in Harlem, he found few female-
headed families.[71]

Oddly, slavery bears little responsibility for today's
explosive African-American illegitimacy rate. In *The End of
Racism*, Dinesh D'Souza says:

> The worst decay in the two-parent black family unit seems
> to have occurred not during slavery or because of slavery, but
> much later and for different reasons. Nor is there any evidence
> that as a consequence of slavery, blacks condoned illegitimacy as
> acceptable within community. For the decline and fragility of the
> contemporary black family, the institution of slavery bears only a
> minor responsibility.[72]

Something has happened to reverse African-Americans'
striving to return to morality. Freedom came to mean
indulgence in drink and drugs and living for the weekend
party. African-American men no longer passionately sought
marriage; African-American women became sex objects to

be lived with and lain with. It has come to be that African-American women live to give birth to a child; marriage can come later, if at all. The fashionable thing now is for young people to listen to lewd music that blasts loudly in their ears, luring them into a life of sex and irresponsible "love." Respect for another is a rare item among African-Americans; the result is a variety of violent acts perpetuated against one another. There exists a thrill for thralldom; African-Americans are dreadfully drifting back into the regions of bondage.

We must continue to teach morality and not only technology. We must teach character and conduct, not condoms, "safe-sex," or "responsible sex," which are but a technical solution. But, how do we solve the moral problem? It is wrong to pursue flesh as if it were heaven. It is wrong to reduce women's importance to their womb, whether it is done through film, movies, or the bed—it's the same thing. You cannot have morality without drawing boundaries.

Criminologists find that even under poor social and economic conditions, churchgoing serves as an insulator against crime and delinquency. These and other findings give evidence of the importance of character formation—teaching the difference between right and wrong and the value of morality.[73]

Look at Def Jam records for an example of how African-Americans humiliate each other, calling each other niggers, dogs, and fools, and reducing African-American women to their genitals. These "music artists" tell jokes that the "oppressor" will never tell, but that the "oppressor" is all too willing to listen to and financially support jokes African-Americans tell about each other. We are laughing at our own demise. What's so sick about all of this is that African-American men and women collaborate in their own oppression. Women sit on the front row laughing while men tell jokes about their genitals. There are no boundaries anymore, and you cannot have morality without drawing boundaries.

ABANDONMENT OF CONTENTMENT

Not only must African-Americans return to Jesus Christ and live up to that call, but we must not leap for the lure, fall for the fake, and dive for the deceptive apples of materialism. We must sing the song of our African-American ancestors who strongly resisted materialism: "You can have this world, but give me Jesus."

Less than fifty years after African-Americans had gained freedom from bondage, weak knees overtook them. Like a weary antelope plodding through a sun-parched wilderness and suddenly coming upon a body of water, African-Americans came out of slavery and happened upon the Lake of Materialism, knelt down, and lapped its addictive liquid until their minds became numbed in drunkenness and their eyes became blinded to the road that lay before them. Materialism quickly became the end sought by African-Americans, rather than the freedom found in Jesus Christ.

While African-Americans coming out of slavery accumulated houses and land, African-Americans today are accumulating clothes and cars. The desire for ownership of land has eroded among us. What we like is to drive, not necessarily own, cars: big cars, little cars, and any kind of car as long as it is a car. The first thing a young African-American boy wants is a car. He longs for this more than anything else. There is an obsession among African-American people for clothes, television sets, radios, stereo consoles, and other material things that wear out, rot and decay. Bernice Dorssett in *From Streets of Gold* writes:

> While in darkness I did many foolish things. Craving only that which I could see, taste or feel. It was while I slept that someone switched the price tag on my soul. Somehow, my cost of living got all mixed up. The items with the highest price tags had no meaning, but the things that made life worth living like love, joy, faith, peace, patience, and giving were tossed in the bargain basement of my soul and labeled "reduced for clearance." Now that my eyes are open and have turned from darkness to light I can see clearly where beautiful things in the bargain basement of my soul belong. So I'm putting all the price tags back in the proper place with Jehovah.[74]

Look at the high rate of suicide. Among White men, it is highest after age 65 when they are declining in health and feel they have no more control over their future. But the highest rate of suicide among African-American males is between the ages of 25-34, when they are young and full of verve. They look ahead but they can't see themselves in the future, and they look within and they see even less.

Obsession with material possessions has often been a deterrent and diversion for people in quest for freedom. "Their end is destruction, their god is the belly, and they glory in their shame, with minds set on earthly things" (Philippians 3:17-19).

As African-Americans, may we once again cast ourselves completely upon the mercy and care of God through Jesus Christ, who will supply all needs (Philippians 4:19) as well as contentment with whatever possessions we have. This is true freedom and a corrective for reversal into materialism.

ABANDONMENT OF INGENUITY

African-Americans must return to their quest for freedom in their efforts to develop businesses and industry. It is too often an untold story that African-American slaves were quite creative and innovative in providing for themselves. Slavery provided few, if any, comforts of life for African-Americans; they taught themselves the way of survival and relative comfort. The need for shoes motivated Jan Matseliger to develop the shoe machine. The need to tell the time of day and understand the changing of the seasons encouraged Benjamin Banneker to create the first American clock and produce an almanac. He also was responsible for laying the design for the nation's capital city, Washington, D.C. Another African-American man, Granville T. Wood, was responsible for developing a communication system through which two train engineers could talk with each other, determining their location and preventing accidents. He also was responsible for the air-brake system that adequately stops trains.

Examples of creativity and innovations in business and industry among African-Americans as a whole exceed that of other groups. On and on go the citations of a people coming out of slavery, fiercely engaged in the labor of business and industry as they strove on their way to freedom. But in the past thirty years, something has happened to turn around the surge in business and industry among African-Americans. Here, too, a great reversal has occurred. Industry among African-Americans, i.e., the development of commodities out of raw materials, is virtually extinct.

Businesses begun toward the end of the 1800s and the beginning of the 1900s have either disappeared or are just holding on to survival by a thread. There is little effort to harness and control the skills unique to African-Americans and develop the skills into corporate efforts that would yield jobs, financial security, and independence for our people. This truly is a great reversal, for it has thrown African-Americans once again upon White people for security, the provision of jobs, and money. It is a new kind of slavery; but it has been caused by African-Americans' failure to follow through on what had been begun by our ancestors. Almost on every hand, African-Americans must turn to outsiders—White people who control businesses and industry—for jobs and financial security. As a result, African-Americans find themselves obligated to and dependent on White people (for example, the NAACP could fold if it had not enjoyed the support of the Jewish community and of labor unions); and African-Americans fail to elicit the respect of those to whom they are obligated. African-Americans need to return to the attitude of independence in labor, business, and industry that characterized their ancestors. They should shun contempt for labor and return to love for labor and independence; this is the way to freedom in Christ.

ABANDONMENT OF COMMUNITY

The passing of the Civil Rights Bill did two things for African-Americans: (1) it knocked down walls of segregation that should not have been erected in the first place; (2) it also created a mad passion for integration, creating an undermining of resources and capacity of the African-American. The result was an erosion of the African-American community's ability to deal with its own problems, since everyone started leaving the community.

The problems of teenage pregnancy, gangs, and crime were

always in the African-American community. These are not new problems; it's the extreme role which these problems have assumed. Some assume that these problems are strange because there is no longer an adequate "Institutional Intervention." Institutional intervention within the African-American community has been nonexistent because the African-Americans who had the resources to build the institutions left the community. These African-Americans find themselves supporting the oppressors' institutions, in order to curry their favor. If a man is not acceptable to himself, how can he be acceptable to anyone else?

I recognize that our problem is both external and internal. I believe a people who cannot deal with themselves internally, who cannot save themselves, are lost forever. Despite the obstacles put in the way of our ancestors by their oppressors, our ancestors' greatest struggle was against themselves: the struggle to avoid contradicting that which was in them—their values, the choices they made for liberation, and their high value for human life.

In earlier days, despite the oppressor, we didn't have the kinds of internal problems that we are having today. Even when laws were passed against our forebears' loving, they found ways to love. When the oppressor stole their husbands, their wives, and their children, ways were found to relocate them. Even when the masters tried to teach them immorality by immoral assault, our ancestors taught their own morality of truth and righteousness. They raised up African-American families in the midst of ruin and created a model for all humanity to follow. No one today can use "hard times" as an excuse for inaction.

ABANDONING OUR DEMAND FOR RESPECT

"Power never concedes anything without a demand. It never has and it never will," said Frederick Douglass. In a 1997 poll, the Joint Center for Political and Economic Studies found former President Clinton to be more popular among African-Americans than either the Reverend Jesse Jackson or General Colin Powell.

I am puzzled: What has President Clinton done for African-Americans but project, unlike any other president in recent memory, his comfort with African-Americans? Or is it, as Reverend Joseph E. Lowery, former president of the Southern Christian Leadership Conference, said, "It's the saxophone; the man has soul." I wonder: maybe this African-American support either amused Bill Clinton or greatly befuddled him. Perhaps he thought: "Why do they love me so? What have I done?" Beyond cabinet and other job appointments that have small impact on the general African-American community, Bill Clinton did discernibly little for African-American people. His positive initiatives may be viewed as largely symbolic.

This should not surprise anyone. No segment of the national electorate has given more to, yet demanded and received less from, the national Democratic Party than African-Americans. We don't take ourselves seriously; therefore no one else does. Can our support for anything, including the Democratic Party, simply be won with gestures? We have to start making specific demands on all political leaders and follow through.

AFRICAN-AMERICANS MUST TAKE CONTROL

Racism, the systematic subordination of one race by another, remains a major problem in the United States for the African-American family. Nevertheless, there is much that African-Americans can do. Instead of resigning ourselves to victim status, it is time for African-Americans to take action, like others in the past. Before affirmative action, the Civil Rights Act of 1964, the Voting Rights Act of 1965, or the Open Housing Act of 1968, Supreme Court justice Robert Jackson wrote in an unpublished 1954 Brown vs. Board of Education draft concurrence, "Negro progress under segregation has been spectacular and most dramatic advances in the annals of man."[75]

African-American Harvard sociologist Orlando Patterson said,

"The sociological truths are that America, while still flawed in its race relations...is now the least racist white-majority society in the world; has a better record of legal protection of minorities than any other society, white or black; offers more opportunities to a greater number of black persons than any other society, including all those of Africa...."[76]

John O. Sullivan, the editor of the *National Review*, put it this way, "White racism exists. But its social power is weak, the social power against it overwhelming." The marketplace punishes racism, he suggests, because racism is against the economic interests of the practitioner.[77]

When some Texaco executives were caught on tape demeaning fellow African-American employees, Texaco's CEO appeared on ABC's *Nightline* to apologize to African-American workers, in particular, and to African-Americans in general. He offered automatic raises to many African-American employees and publicly promised to settle the lawsuit. Why? Because Texaco lost $1 billion in shareholder value in two days and had many irate customers—African-

American and non-African-American—preparing to cut up their credit cards unless and until Texaco did something. They did. Fast. Real fast. Racism is bad for business.

In 1901, Booker T. Washington, a former slave, said this:

> When a Negro girl learns to cook, to wash dishes, to sew, to write a book, or a Negro boy learns to groom horses, or to grow sweet potatoes, or to produce butter, or to build a house, or to be able to practice [sic] medicine, as well or better than someone else, they will be rewarded regardless of race or colour [sic]. In the long run, the world is going to have the best, and any difference in race, religion, or previous history will not long keep the world from what it wants.
>
> I think that the whole future of my race hinges on the question as to whether or not it can make itself of such indispensable value that the people in the town and the state where we reside will feel that our presence is necessary to the happiness and well-being of the community. No man who continues to add something to the material, intellectual, and moral-well being of the place in which he lives is long left without proper reward. This is a great human law, which cannot be permanently nullified.[78]

William Raspberry, columnist for *The Washington Post*, echoes some of Washington's sentiments:

> A myth has crippled African-America, the myth that racism is the dominant influence in our lives. Two things flow from this racism-all myth. It puts the solution to our difficulties outside our control. And it encourages the fallacy that attacking racism as the source of our problems is the same as attacking our problems.[79]

Racism does exist, and all of its attendant evils have thrown roadblocks into the path toward success for African-Americans. But this attitude of African-Americans—"We must wait for White America to get its moral act together before we can do anything about racism and its impact on African-American families and communities" — must be challenged.

Most of the obstacles facing African-Americans are both internal and external. They will not yield to a simple one-sided solution. All too often, internal despair makes common cause with external injustice and oppression. If external forces and personalities think that African-Americans are inferior and treat them like some subhuman, inferior group of people, that is external discrimination. But if African-Americans believe that they are inferior and behave as if they are inferior, by acting foolish, wasting their time, throwing away their money, neglecting their families or themselves, forsaking their church and community, and having illegitimate children, that is internal, self-inflicted disablement and disaster.

Neither racism nor the lack of money plays the biggest role in the dysfunctional development of African-American children. Caring, loving parents remain the greatest factor in creating a self-reliant, upwardly mobile, confident adult. For example, in 1987, a wealthy, idealistic philanthropist in Philadelphia "adopted" 112 inner-city sixth-grade kids, most of whom were products of broken homes. The philanthropist, George Weiss, guaranteed a fully-funded education up through college if only the kids would refrain from drugs, unwedded motherhood or fatherhood, and crime. He even provided tutors, workshops, after-school programs, summer programs, and counselors to be available when trouble arose, whether personal or otherwise.

Thirteen years later, how many of these kids successfully made it to college and beyond? Forty-five never made it through high school. Of these, thirty-five dropped out, one died while in school, four died after dropping out, four are working on a GED, and one graduated trade school.[80]

Of the high school graduates, thirteen are four-year-college graduates; eleven are enrolled in four-year colleges; five are enrolled in two-year colleges; twelve have dropped out of two- and four-year colleges; seven graduated trade school; eight are enrolled in trade school; six dropped out of trade school; and five graduates pursued no further education.

Of the sixty-seven boys, nineteen have grown into adult felons. Among the forty-five girls, they had sixty-three children, and more than half had their babies before the age of eighteen.

If you took more than a hundred kids from similar backgrounds, but no guaranteed education, the results would have been approximately the same. What do we make of this? The answer is simple: it isn't about money, it's about values. It's about discipline and application. It's about character, about working hard when you don't want to. And these values are instilled in the home. A constant stomping out of racism is a must, but there also has to be a call back to personal morality.

CONCLUSION

It's not easy for a wayward people to make an about-face and get back on the road that leads to freedom in Christ. It will not be easy for America, nor will it be easy for African-Americans. There is always the deterrent of self-doubt. Often it is easier to resign oneself to the situation someone else puts us in. Thomas Jefferson resigned himself to American slavery by insisting that King George of England was responsible for slavery by permitting ship lines to engage in transporting African slaves.

African-Americans have spent a great deal of time

pointing out how White people have been responsible for African-Americans being the way they are. Thus, developing independence in business, industry, and jobs is thwarted. It will not be easy for White Americans or African-Americans to make the turnabout, for these and other kinds of impediments and obstacles are in the way. But if Christian freedom is to be realized, the effort must be made.

Our African ancestors not only chide us but they also cheer us to get back to the road that leads to ultimate freedom and to stay on that road. *Stay on the road!* With Paul, our African forefathers remind us that it is not one's self or one's own power and ingenuity that keep the traveler on the road to freedom: "God is at work in you, both to will and to work for his good pleasure" (Philippians 2:13).

If we cease and desist from traveling the road to freedom and turn back to a previous state of bondage, we are saying to God, in whom our forefathers placed complete trust, "you are unable to give the strength and will to complete the race." Such is not the case.

The one thing the African-American church in the small community of Belleview did for me was to heighten my awareness that Jesus has not left African-Americans alone in suffering. He is not only with them, building them up where they are torn down and propping them up on every tilting side, but he is also coming on the clouds of heaven to take them home to glory.

In Jesus' death and resurrection, God has freed us to fight against social and political structures while not being limited by them. I remember our African-American preacher expressing this truth with apocalyptic imagination:

I know the way gets awful dark; sometimes it looks like
Everything is against us. Sometimes we wake up in the

Dark hours of midnight, briny tears flowing down our cheeks
Crying and not knowing what we are crying about. But
Because God is our Captain and is on board now, we can
Sit still and hear the word of the Lord. Away back before
The wind ever blew or before the earth was made, our God
Had us in mind. He looked down through time one morning
And saw you and me and ordained from the very beginning
that we should be his children. You remember old John
the Revelator who claimed he saw a number that had
come through hard trails and great tribulations and who
had washed their robes in the blood of he Lamb. Oh,
Brothers! Ain't you glad that you have already been in
the dressing room, because it won't be long before we will
take the wings of the morning and go where there will be no
more sin and sorrow, no more weeping and mourning.

God is the Sovereign ruler and nothing can thwart his will
to liberate the oppressed. God gives security to the oppressed
(Psalm 12:5), protecting the weak from the strong and the
poor from the oppressor (Psalm 35:10). He is a God who cares
for orphans and widows, who gives the lonely a home to live
in and who leads prisoners in to freedom (Psalm 68:5-6). He
secures justice for the poor and upholds the cause of needy
(Psalm 140:12). He upholds the cause of the oppressed and
gives food to the hungry. The Lord sets prisoners free; the
Lord gives sight to the blind. The Lord lifts up those who are
bowed down, the Lord loves the righteous (Psalm 146:6-8).

12 What African-American Churches Need to Hear

Kenneth R. Greene

The African-American church must address the challenges of African-Americans. How well the church accepts and knows the divine mandate will determine its own image in the eyes of the struggling African-American masses and the degree to which America will be humanely shaped. If the church fails, it will lose its divine credentials.

The general task of the African-American church is the liberation of African-Americans. The African-American church has the responsibility and opportunity in a time of great need, not only to do more of what it has done in the past for the African-American community survival, but also to shift its emphasis from African-American survival to African-American liberation.

God is the God of liberation. His many acts of liberation in Scripture culminated in his sending Jesus into the world. When Jesus came, he explained his mission to humanity by using the words of the prophet Isaiah. He opened the scroll and read:

The Spirit of the Lord is on me, because he has anointed me to preach good news to the poor. He has sent me to proclaim freedom for the prisoners and recovery of sight for the blind, to release the oppressed, to proclaim the year of the Lord's favor. (Luke 4:18f.)

The African-American church must liberate African-Americans from the many crises they face. All Americans suffer some setbacks and face challenges that threaten their existence. African-Americans are vulnerable because they lack the resources and support systems necessary to meet the challenges that all peoples face. Therefore, it is important to challenge the church, God's people, to manage well the natural vicissitudes of life.

At this point, I want to look at one of many crises African-Americans are facing, its consequences and implications for the church, and to offer some possible solutions. The measure of the church's ministry to African-Americans will determine the quality of its own mission.

ECONOMIC DEVELOPMENT

There is a great misconception about the role and influence of the African-American church in its community. Any previous influence is in decline. It is now time for the African-American church to take a proactive position within its community. Through its programs, emphasis should be placed on encouragement, support, and a genuine interest shown in the affairs of the community. Programs designed to help build self-confidence, to aid in skills development, and to provide opportunities for economic development are essential for community survival.

The area of economics reveals for African-Americans some of the greatest obstacles in racism. Racism is any attitude, action, or institutional structure that subordinates a person or group because of their color or race. Racism is not just a matter of attitude. The actions of individuals or institutional structures can also contribute to the many forms of racism. Moreover, racism involves having the power to carry out systematic, discriminatory practices through the institutions of our society. Power plus prejudice equals racism.

Because of racism, a growing number of African-Americans have become irrelevant to the U.S. economy. The level of permanent unemployment for African-Americans under the age of 25 has reached the staggering level of more than 42% and continues to climb.

The most powerful argument for the inevitability of Whites' genocide of African-Americans is Sidney M. Wilhelm's *Who Needs the Negro?* He says:

> The life situation of Black Americans deteriorates with the passing of each year..., technological efficiency makes possible the full realization of the nation's anti-Negro beliefs. The arrival of automation eliminates the need for Black labor, and racist values call for the Negro's removal from the American scene...as the races pull apart into lifestyles with greater polarity, the Black ghetto evolves into the equivalent of the Indian reservation. "What is the point," demands White America, "in tolerating an unwanted racial minority for acceptance?" With machines now replacing human labor, who needs the Negro?[81]

The most fundamental economic reality for African-Americans is that they are being removed from the labor market where they are immersed in the economics of uselessness.

The answer to the question of why there are so many homes without fathers might be found in the unemployment rates. More than three million African-American men cannot find work, or are working and not making enough money to sustain a family. That inability to support family, experts say, is the single most important reason why many African-American men never marry. Children however, continue to be born.[82]

As a consequence of homes without a father, some of the internal capacity to protect, to nurture, and to transmit values to the children is lost. Children should learn about relationships, responsibility, and partnership. But if the father is not in the home, regardless of the reason, children sometimes view this situation as *normal* and, in years to come, are likely to display the same lack of responsibility when it comes to their own children. This trend must be changed, and it can be. But it is going to take the strongest upsurge of support the church has ever displayed. If this fight is lost, then everything is lost.

The African-American church must find ways to provide full employment, for we cannot have wholesome relationships if we cannot provide for each other. We cannot expect African-American men standing on the street corner all day to be productive partners, and we cannot expect teen girls who drop out of school in order to have babies to form long-term relationships either. We've got to find ways to help African-Americans achieve some economic stability in their lives.

Economic factors are very important in developing relationships. Many African-American women do not have men because almost half of the African-American men are not working and, therefore, are not desirable as husbands. And yet the children are still born.

Economic genocide cripples the African-American male's ego; his self-esteem is lost, he cannot compete with the welfare laws, and he is unable to be the provider, protector, producer, and nurturer of his home. Thus, a growing number of men turn their backs on their wives and children. The African-American family is weaker as a result.

Female households with no spouse present comprise 76 percent of all poor African-American families, compared with 48 percent of poor Hispanic families and 44 percent of poor White families. About five in ten African-American families with a female householder and no husband were in poverty in 1999. Many children have never seen anyone in their family get up and go to work.[83]

Preachers escalate African-American men's frustrations and irritations when they come to worship; our men come and sit for three hours through song after song, and announcement after announcement, with someone asking them (more than once) for money that they don't have, and surrounded by people who are neither seriously trying to commune with the divine presence nor concerned about their unemployment.

THE NEW TESTAMENT CHURCH: WHAT DID IT DO?

The New Testament church had to deal with economic genocide. What did it do? According to Acts 2:44-45: "Now all who believed were together, and had all things in common and sold their possessions and goods and divided them among all, as anyone had need." Again in Acts 4:32-35:

Now the multitude of those who believed were of one heart and one soul; neither did anyone say that any of the things he possessed was his own, but they had all things in common; nor was there anymore among them who lacked; for all who were possessors of lands or houses sold them and brought the proceeds of the things that were sold and laid them at the apostles' feet; they distributed to each as anyone had need.

These passages stress the common mind and the generosity of the disciples in their life together. The gift of the Spirit (4:31) led not only to inspired preaching but also to Christian fellowship and generosity. "No one claimed that any of his possessions was his own, but they shared everything they had." Notice they did not say that nothing belonged to them; the text says they didn't *claim* belongings—they owned them but they did not claim them as their possessions.

Today we not only own possessions, but we claim them. We have exercised exclusive rights in those things that God has given us to manage. We need to understand that God has given resources to us, but we are responsible for sharing those to help accomplish the mission.

The early church was not only sharing their God, but they were sharing their goods. With the economic situation in Palestine steadily deteriorating because of famine and political unrest, employment was limited not only for Galileans and others who had left their fishing and farming for life in the city, but also for the regular residents of Jerusalem who now faced economic and social sanctions because of their new messianic faith.

Each of the early disciples regarded his private estate as being at the community's disposal: those who possessed houses and lands sold these in order that they might be more conveniently available to the community in the form of money. The richer members made provision for the poorer, and for a time, no one had any room to complain of hunger or want.

In view of such a combination of social concern and proclamation of the Word, it is no wonder Luke goes on to say "and much grace was upon them all."

African-Americans have no businesses or industries to

provide jobs for themselves. We are dangerously at the economic mercy of White America. If the African-American church is going to sustain its freedom and the freedom of its people, it must be economically strong and economically independent. No other denominational expression of the Christian faith in America demonstrates economic dependence on outside assistance, be it sacred or secular, as does the African-American church. Yet, the fact is that the African-American church, with all of its wealth, is failing to support those institutions that provide education and health care for its people and is failing to utilize its economic resources to provide jobs for its constituents.

The African-American church has to address this economic genocide. African-American men need money, job opportunities, business resources, and relevant skill training. The African-American church collects money, but it does little to create opportunities through which it can make more money.

If the African-American church ever loses its economic freedom, it can never be a service to its people—the poor and oppressed. The African-American church must remain economically solvent, strong, independent, and free. The early church was economically independent; and because it was, it was free.

The early church possessed a strong sense of brotherhood and therefore a feeling of obligation concerning their mutual needs. Fellowship expressed something new and independent. The individual was completely upheld by the community. There was an independent revolutionary element in Christianity. Its economic independence allowed it to wage its pretentious battle to establish Christianity in a cruel world without fear of intimidation or reprisal from unfavorable contributors. The early church not only had to claim its freedom, to prepare itself faithfully for the long road to freedom, and to do this in the context of unity; it also had to be economically strong and independent. Therefore, it truly was free.

COOPERATIVES

Several churches today are demonstrating what African-American churches could do by marshaling their economic resources. African-American churches have to help themselves if they want to become self-sufficient. The church, as one of the most stable institutions in our community, has to take the lead in making sure our people stay afloat.

More and more churches are embarking on business ventures designed to breathe economic life into ailing African-American communities. The ministers leading these new church enterprises maintain that bringing economic stability to depressed communities is as much a part of the Lord's work as preaching on Sunday mornings.

So if housing and jobs are concerns in the community, the church has the responsibility to address itself to those needs. The church is the one institution that can help an economic turnaround happen. It is up to the African-American church to show our people that we can control our own destinies. If not the African-American church, who?

The individual African-American male cannot compete with the government, which has all these little silly laws that make it cheaper for two persons to live together in an adulterous relationship than to marry; when or if they enter into a legitimate marriage, the government increases their rent by reducing their subsidies. The government, through its oppressive tactics, encourages illicit relationships and illegitimate births, and then blames the victims for their victimization.

The African-American church can help solve this problem by finding houses with low or no back taxes, buying them, and completely rehabilitating them for low income African-Americans. Ownership of land is a basis of economic power. The matter of land and the relationship of African-American people to land have considerable significance both for the social health of the general society and also for the African-American community's own welfare. The church's ownership of a part of Mother Earth can provide a land base for the community.

A charge has been leveled at the African-American church that it has wasted too much money constructing church buildings to satisfy the ego needs of the pastor or the congregation. Perhaps the church needs to be revolutionary in its thinking and start having contractors build church buildings, lease them from the contractors, and then use the millions of dollars that would go into constructing a building to purchase land, houses, and businesses. This type of business foresight will prove to be the economic anchor for the African-American community.

The African-American church must tell its people not to buy homes in cities where they cannot work, to boycott banks which discriminate against African-Americans in access to credit, to boycott stores which refuse to employ African-Americans while serving African-American trade, and to boycott public service corporations which practice racial discrimination.

The African-American church must create businesses in its community and deposit the income in African-American owned banks, and African-American produced products must be placed on the counters of all their stores. This will help stop the drain of resources out of the African-American community with nothing remaining there for its rehabilitation.

The African-American church needs to embark on business ventures designed to breathe economic life into ailing African-American communities, projects such as (1) developing a multi-purpose social service agency that handles everything from medical needs to counseling; (2) developing credit unions; (3) purchasing neighborhood shopping centers; (4) and purchasing service stations.

One of the greatest problems facing African-Americans is mis-education, i.e., African-Americans are continually being prepared for services that are no longer marketable.

The African-American church's economic standing with the race is directly proportional to the race's level of educational and moral development. Improvement in education and moral development for the African-American community will result in economic improvement for the church. Education and civil rights are necessary conditions for economic development. Education is the fundamental ingredient in the prescription for saving our children and our communities. The African-American church must support learning and supplement the work of schools through tutoring, volunteer work, monitoring, and encouraging increased parental involvement.

THE AFRICAN-AMERICAN CHURCH'S DIRECTION AND CHARACTER

While there is a general consensus as to the prominent role of the African-American church in the community, there is debate over the direction and character of its influence. In the past, sociologists and social scientists advanced three models of the African-American church and its role in alleviating conditions for African-Americans. The Assimilation-Isolation Model views the African-American church as an obstruction to the complete assimilation and integration of African-Americans into (European) American Society.[84] By socially segregating their members, African-American churches impede their level of participation in other voluntary and civic associations and activities. Frazier, a leading proponent of the Assimilation-Isolation Model, feels that as African-Americans achieve higher socioeconomic status and assimilation into White American society, the traditional role of the African-American church as a spiritual and social refuge will cease to exist.[85]

The Compensatory Model asserts that the church is a significant presence in African-American communities by virtue of its position as the primary voluntary association of African-Americans. Through the church as a functioning and viable community organization, African-Americans have the opportunity to learn organizational skills and participate in a variety of roles typically denied them in wider society. This model differs from the Assimilation-Isolation Model in that it conveys a basically positive attitude toward the African-American church. However, to a large extent the African-American family and other African-American institutions, such as the church, are viewed as reactions to discrimination and segregation, and as such are portrayed as maladaptation.[86]

Similar to the Compensatory Model, the Ethnic Community Model emphasizes the role of the African-American church for enhancing individual self-worth and building a functional community that is based on a sense of group identity and collective interest.[87] Consistent with this model is the observation that churches serve as institutional bases during struggles against racial injustice.

These differing models of the nature and role of the African-American church are limited by their over-emphasis on a single dimension of church functioning, which consequently obscures its multifaceted roles. The African-American church has had multiple roles and functions in the life of the African-American community. The African-American church has helped African-Americans personally and socially. On an individual level, the church promotes general positive feelings, sustains and strengthens, provides personal assistance, and provides guidelines for moral behavior and personal conduct. On the communal level, the church is a source of unity, a community gathering place, and active in attaining specific goals or achieving social purposes for African-Americans. Spiritual help reflects the church's role in promoting increased religious activity or in meeting spiritual and religious goals and needs.[88] The church has always performed multiple functions for its people.

Never has the responsibility of the African-American church been so crucial as it is today. Yet it could evade its God-given role by being too misdirected, too timid, and too brainwashed. Without taking seriously its Lord's mandate, it could become a closed, self-serving, institutionalized, good-feeling society dedicated to sanctifying the status quo on Sunday morning instead of healing the broken-hearted, applying the gospel to the poor, and working for the liberation of the hurt and enslaved. The mission, the role, the function of the African-American church is determined by Scripture and not by sociologists and social scientists, though these experts are very resourceful in assisting the African-American church in determining what the needs of its people are.

The African-American church has the responsibility and the opportunity in a time of great need to do more of what it has done in the past for the African-American community, but it also has the awesome mandate to make a shift of emphasis from "survival" to "liberation." To do this, the church, through its outreach programs, must become a provider of job opportunities and a vehicle for developing entrepreneurial skills. Thankfully, some churches are doing this. For example, Pastor Kirbyjon Caldwell of Houston, Texas—the nationally recognized minister of the largest United Methodist church in the United States—after he became a minister in 1982, ambitiously developed a plan that espouses a holistic approach to a variety of civic needs. The plan calls for 452 new homes, a YMCA, an elementary school, an independent-living community, two five-acre business parks, a commercial catfish pond, a state-of-the-art tennis center, a family life center, a prayer center, a neighborhood park, and an amphitheater. Eighty percent of the homes are targeted for low-to moderate-income families. His best selling book, *The Gospel of Good Success*, published in 1999 by Simon & Schuster, outlines a step-by-step approach to spiritual and economic empowerment. Caldwell says, "If you do what you've always done, you're going to get what you've always gotten. I've never let what I've never done stop me from doing something different."[89]

Hartford Avenue Baptist Church in Detroit has developed a multi-purpose social service agency that handles everything from medical needs to counseling. The church also runs a print shop (the only African-American bindery in the state of Michigan), an auto shop, a 460-pupil school, and a $2 million credit union.[90]

The projects undertaken by these churches are vast and

varied. The ministers leading these new church enterprises maintain that fostering economic stability is a part of their ministries. That means that whatever needs people have, the church and the preacher should be involved in helping meet them. So if housing and jobs are concerns in the community, the church has a responsibility to address itself to those needs. The African-American church is the one institution that can help an economic turnaround happen. The church should weave its way into the economic fabric of the community in which it is situated. It is up to the African-American church to show our people that we can control our own destinies. If not the African-American church, who?

In the area of cooperation, the African-American church can affirm the liberation of the African-American community through demonstrating the value of churches cooperating with one another. Every church in the community does not need a day care program, a family life center, a food co-op, etc. The entire community could be better served with single-unit efforts. When church members observe the results of the cooperative endeavors coming from the pastors, they will begin to see and understand what results can be produced when people cooperate. There is a very real need for more pastors to demonstrate a willingness to be cooperative.

In the area of community support, pastors should encourage and practice support of African-American enterprises. Too often, the African-American church acquires its goods and services from non-African-American vendors. Its dollars, its church monies need to turn over more times in its own communities than is now the reality. In addition, it needs to hold African-American businesses to the same standards as it holds White enterprises.

The African-American pastor, if the race is to be revived,

must begin to address those issues that affect the quality of life in the community. The preacher can ill afford not to address the issues of ecology, peace, and justice, etc. It is clear that when the pastor calls attention to issues, the membership will begin to respond. The pastor should lead the demand for honesty and integrity among African-American officials rather than yelling "racism" when someone is caught with his or her hand in the proverbial cookie jar. The church must demand a higher standard than what seems to be accepted now.

It may be appropriate to consider the role of theological education and its impact on the African-American community. Emphasis should be on the place and role of the professional African-American theological school within the African-American community of faith. The African-American seminary should begin to take an active interest in the community. For example, several institutions around the Atlanta University Center have designed programs for assisting the public housing arena. The seminary needs to be in the midst of this attempt to reclaim positive life. There is an aspect of the theological curriculum that is known as Practical Theology, with emphasis on the word "practical." It is necessary for the African-American seminary to meet the requirements of the accreditation agencies. However, the seminary must also be responsive to the needs of its other constituencies, and this suggests a need to rethink its curriculum. Attention needs to be focused on teaching creative thought rather than modeling students to fit a certain pre-designed model. There is more to the African-American church than preaching.

African-American youth are being lost because they lack motivation. Where are the how-to seminars that teach students to do real Christian work in the community? It appears that fieldwork assignments tend to be given with little forethought and virtually no afterthought. Yet, there are countless churches in the African-American community that could be helped by having the presence of one person who has some seminary-based theological training. The biblical assertion that "the harvest is plentiful, but the laborers are few" is accurate as applied to the African-American seminary-trained people found working within the African-American church.

CONCLUSION

The African-American church has been the central axis around which the rest of the community revolves. For over a century, it has served as a refuge for African-Americans from racial discrimination, social oppression, and economic exploitation. The African-American church must continue to develop ways to build bridges into this segment of the community or otherwise the poverty-related problems faced by its people will continue to erode the family's effectiveness, its purpose, and its mission.

The African-American is depreciated and relegated to the margins of family life and influence. He is not able to provide and nurture his family like the White man. Until the oppressor removes his foot from the African-American man's neck, the African-American man will not be able to assert his spiritual strength and demonstrate his sense of responsibility and ethnic pride, much less the redemptive purpose of God in the world.

If the African-American man cannot be the redemptive force in is own family, how do we expect him to proclaim God's redemptive plan in the world? Attitudes are critical in the successful implementation of any African-American family reflecting the image of God in the world. One thing affecting the African-American man's attitude and not the white man's attitude is economic oppression.

The economic realities tend to exacerbate all other problems, such as health care, education, and housing. In order to cope, many African-American fathers have turned to crime to survive instead of turning to God. If the African-American family is still basically struggling with the necessities of life, God's redemptive purpose in the world cannot be successfully achieved. As a matter of fact, the redemptive purpose of God will never be experienced in the African-American family itself. It is continuing to struggle to find the resources to provide, protect, and nurture itself. Sanity, health, and wholeness are inherent in the African-American family's redemptive purpose. Family life in any form of oppressed conditions can become pathological instead of redemptive.

Racism has been and still is a powerful foe. Unlike the African-American father, the White American father can provide some economic security so that parental energies can be dispensed into creating a redemptive atmosphere in the home. When African-American fathers must expend most of their concerns on their economic survival, much of the energy needed to provide psychological support for the family is depleted.

Much more could be said, but it is clear that though African-Americans, as a people, can survive the racial crisis they face, their survival depends on African-Americans' willingness to change their mindset. They must assume responsibility for themselves. African-Americans can no longer look for salvation from beyond themselves. Our salvation rests with ourselves and within ourselves. African-Americans must begin to rise up against those who would keep them enslaved to welfare, regardless of the color, sex, or political agendas.

13   What White Churches & Institutions Need to Hear

Kenneth R. Greene

O God,
Maker of every thing and judge of all that you have made,
From the dust of the earth you have formed us and
From the dust of death you would raise us up.
By the redemptive power of the cross, create in us clean
Hearts and put within us a new spirit, that we may
Repent of our sins and lead lives worthy of your
Calling; through Jesus Christ our Lord. Amen.
—Laurence Hull Stookey, *Ash Wednesday Prayer*[91]

In his book *The Trouble With Friendship: Why Americans Can't Think Straight About Race*, Benjamin DeMott notes that America's problems with race appear to be solved, at least at the movies, one-to-one.[92] From *Pulp Fiction* to *The Little Princess*, whenever Whites and African-Americans meet one another on film, they are the best of friends, part of the common humanity. One of the most touching aspects (the only touching aspect?) of *Pulp Fiction* is the charming camaraderie between two murderers, one African-American, one White-American. In *White Men Can't Jump*, a courageous White man, struggling to survive on the mean basketball courts of downtown Los Angeles, is befriended by an understanding African-American protector, played by Wesley Snipes. This film was released the same year as the L.A. riots.

See? We do not really have a racial problem in America. Look how we all get along in film: *Driving Miss Daisy, Forrest Gump, The Shawshank Redemption, Philadelphia, The Power of One, Places in the Heart, Sister Act*—one could go on. Friendship in black and white dominates our movies.[93]

As DeMott notes, such films mask the hard facts. Black infants die in America at twice the rate of white infants. One out of every two black children lives below the poverty line (as compared with one out of seven white children). Nearly four times as many black families exist below the poverty line as white families. More than 50 percent of African-American families have income below $25,000. Among black youths under age twenty, death by murder occurs nearly ten times as often as among whites. Over 60 percent of births to black mothers occur out of wedlock, more than four times the rate for white mothers. The net worth of the typical white household is ten times that of the typical black household. In many states, five to ten times as many blacks as whites aged eighteen to thirty are in prison.[94]

There's quite a gap between Hollywood and Harlem, quite a distance between where I live and my mornings with Jane Clayson nudging her good buddy Bryant Gumbel, reassuring me that we are all really in this together after all. The message of Hollywood sells because it is a message we are desperate to believe: One day long ago, we had a problem with racism, but now that problem has been solved. White people didn't like African-American people back then; therefore, Whites felt guilt and African-Americans capitalized upon White guilt to win certain entitlements. Whites had to cough up the cash for welfare, Head Start, and affirmative action. Finally,

Whites came to the realization that they really did like African-Americans after all. Their guilt was lifted. Therefore, the expenditure of all that money is no longer needed.

Watching *Do the Right Thing*, some White Americans felt quite good about how far, with the help of Spike Lee, they had come since the bad old days of racism; here are nice, hard-working African-American youth in a White-owned pizza parlor. Then comes the scene in which an African-American man at last rises up and beats his White oppressor senseless, and the audience came alive, yelling encouragement, and applauding approvingly. Whites then realized the depth of resentment among African-Americans toward White-sponsored cinematic lies.

The subplot of our national fantasy is this: Here are all these well-meaning White people, with the open hand of friendship extended to all of these African-American people. Fortunately, some enlightened African-American people return the favor and become friends with the Whites, even protect them (as in *Grand Canyon*) from the evils of their less enlightened brothers in the ghetto who want only to rip off the Whites' cars. The image is so appealing because it is offered without cost, without mention or ownership of our sordid past, and coated with thick sentimentality, which always helps things go down easier in Hollywood.

Consider former President George Bush's nomination of Clarence Thomas for the Supreme Court. George Bush told a great public lie when he said that Clarence Thomas was the best available person he could find for nomination to the Supreme Court. Of course, we all knew that was a lie, but few named it for what it was. What George Bush should have said was that "America is still a Society that suffers from a hard history of slavery, and the development of racism is part of our national experience. Accordingly, it is important to appoint African-Americans to positions of power where they can protect other African-Americans from the racism that is still endemic to our society." George Bush did not tell us that, not because he is venial, though he may be, but because the White people do not want to know the truth. They elect their leaders on the basis of whatever fantasies they happen to have at the moment, and their leaders promise to confirm them in their fantasies.

One thing Whites do not want to do is the one thing they need to do: that is, to set their desires within the context of history. Abstracted from a larger account of who they are, what they have done, and where they are going, certain things appear good in themselves. After all, what could possibly be amiss in a BellSouth TV commercial that shows an African-American child, then a White child, then an African-American child, and then a White child singing in harmony, "I am the keeper of the world"? What is wrong is the way Whites use such well-meaning, sentimental gestures to relieve themselves of their responsibility. Despite his own eloquent testimonial to the value of affirmative action, Whites seem determined to use Colin Powell in this project. "Look at Colin Powell," they love to say to their African-American friends and themselves. "He made it. You don't hear him whining on TV." Though Whites' asking price for the perception of equality is rather high—Powell's leadership of the killing in Iraq—they are thrilled to point to visible evidence that the playing field is level and that they are at last ready for an African-American man in the White House. So what is the problem?

DeMott charges Whites with culture-wide evasion. But what are they, as White-Americans, supposed to do? What is wrong with a story that claims that all we need to do is to reach out with an open hand to see that, after all, we're fairly much the same—we're all human beings after all, aren't we? DeMott says our current racial fantasy, which sees racism as a personal problem of bad feelings, miniaturizes and moralizes. Our temptation is to make history irrelevant. "White Americans," says Bill Clinton, "are gripped by the isolation of their own experience. Too many simply have no friends of other races."[95] Whites' racial salvation, it would appear, comes when they are all able to say, "Some of my best friends are Black," a statement thoroughly mocked back in the sixties, (and it should have been).

African-Americans are not immune to the same delusion. In postmodern fashion, by giving up on large, political solutions, Pulitzer Prize winner (for *Elbow Room*) James Alan McPherson urges us to take the only possible steps, the safest steps…small ones, toward a universal culture.[96] Universal cultures, like common humanity or universal human rights, are code words for forgetting history.

Having no larger story that enables them truthfully to tell their story, Whites attempt amnesia. We thus make the present situation of White-Americans and African-Americans in this country into something strange and crazy. Why can't we all just get along; after all, aren't we all in the same boat, aren't we all human beings? Why can't we just forget caste and race and join hands and sing, "We Are the World"?

The current attacks on affirmative action are, in great part, an attempt to deny history. These attacks act as if that mythical level playing field had been achieved, so that all that African-Americans need now do is quit whining and join hands with all well-meaning Whites, who are ready to forgive and to forget. To admit our history might mean to admit that we did not arrive here overnight, so our solutions will not come overnight. A first step would be for Whites to own their history, for White-Americans to admit to their historic entitlements, and for Whites to admit that there are good reasons — historic, economic, and political reasons — why the myth of African-American and White-American sameness is a lie.

Current appeals for one-on-one friendliness as the key to what ails us are based, at least in Hollywood, on a dangerous suppression of differences. First, we must all shed our history, our language, and anything else that makes us uniquely us; then we can be friends.

But our past, in black and white, is not just a matter of a few negative people who refused to get along, but an entrenched, established caste structure. We can see how arduous the road ahead is when we realize that not only did Thomas Jefferson, author of the Declaration of Independence, own slaves, but also that racism was (surely unwittingly) built right into the Constitution.

Perhaps the very first thing we need to do as White-Americans and as individual members of society is to confront our past and see it for what it is. It is a past filled with some of the ugliest possible examples of racial brutality and degradation in human history. We need to recognize it for what it was and is and not explain it away, excuse it, or justify it. Having done that, we should then make a good-faith effort to turn our history around so that we can see it in front of us, so that we can avoid doing what we have done for so long.[97]

Our past tells us that we are not members of a universal human culture, in which some of us just happen to be White and others just happen to be Black. We have a past. The question is, "How is it possible to live together despite our past? How is it possible to be honest about our past?"

Christians live by the conviction that without some means of telling our story in a truthful way, honesty is impossible and the past is not only irretrievable but also invincible. In the season of Lent, a great deal of time is spent on repentance. Repentance does not come naturally. It involves learning a story and practicing rituals that are not a normal part of universal human culture. Repentance means many things, and one meaning is realizing, on the basis of the story of Jesus' temptation, that some goods offered to us in the name of justice or human betterment, are downright satanic (See the meaning attributed to Christ's third temptation in Dostoevsky's *The Brothers Karamazov*, for example). Repentance, as John the Baptist reminds us, involves doing specific, concrete political and economic acts as signs of our turning toward God (Luke 3:7-18).

Repentance, in the current context of American race relations, means to admit that we have a past; it means to be honest about our history. Paul loved to tell his history in places like Galatians. Paul recounted his past, not only because it made his conversion all the more remarkable but also because telling his past was itself an integral part of conversion, turning, *metanoia*.

Yet where do we find the strength for honesty, particularly honesty about that which is most painful in our past, especially the past that still determines us but was not immediately of our own doing? Here I am thinking of all those Whites who say things like, "I never owned a slave. My great-grandfather didn't even own a slave, so why should I feel guilty?" You should feel guilty, simply because you have been fooled by such illusions to believe that because you did not participate directly in the enforcing prejudices, somehow you are excused. You do not actually feel as though you are exercising the power that results in victimizing African-Americans. You do participate, however, even when others exercise this power for you in ways that are to your benefit.

Some of your great-grandfathers did own slaves, and I could tell you that it is a hard history to get over, particularly with the limited means given you by this culture. What you need in order to be truthful is some means of facing the facts without either hating yourselves for your past or hating those who remind you of it.

What's the truth? Racism, the systematic subordination of one race, remains a major problem in the United States for the African-American family. Again, racism is any attitude, action, or institutional structure that subordinates a person or group because of their color or race. Racism is not just a matter of attitudes; actions and institutional structures can also be a form of racism.[98]

Racism involves having the power to carry out systematic discriminatory practices through the institutions of our society. Racism is defined as prejudice plus power. That being true, the obvious question is, "Who's got the power?" And the answer is equally obvious. In the United States, only one racial group has the power to impose its will upon and exploit other racial groups. Only one racial group has the power to pretend that racism does not exist. Therefore, in the United States, the truth that we must face is that racism is White-Americans' problem, and only a White problem.[99]

Does *White Racism* mean that every White person is racist? Yes, every White person is part of the problem, but not necessarily with personal racist intent. We are assuming that most White Americans do not want to be racist, even though every White person participates in and benefits from the system of racism, even if it is against their will.

How can Whites be free? How can your gestures of friendship be saved from being just one more means of elaborate self-delusion ("Some of my best friends are African-American")? Stop trying to solve the wrong problem. For years, you have been trying to change the wrong people. With the best of intentions, you were aiming in the wrong direction. Almost all of our nation's social and political initiatives for solving racial problems attempt to change the victims of racism and the conditions within their communities. In doing so, they avoid the real issue. Concerned people, in the firm belief that racial problems must be solved and racial conflicts reconciled, have devoted time, effort, and money to help African-Americans with their problems. The White churches, the government, the universities, and many other groups work hard to help change African-Americans. Your assumption is that if you pour enough money into changing the victims of racism, they will catch up with you and will achieve a state of equality. But it isn't happening. Why? You are trying to change the wrong people.

The racial problem of the United States is not a minority problem. It is a majority problem. The cause is in the White society. The effects are felt in the communities of African-Americans. The problems of African-Americans are only the symptoms of White America's sickness. The White society owns the racial ghettos of America. They control them, maintain them, and condone them. The institutions and agencies of White America determine what happens there in the ghetto.

The commission reported that the major cause of urban unrest was racism in the White society. This report caused a furor among White-Americans:

What white Americans have never fully understood—but what the Negro can never forget—is that the white society is deeply implicated in the ghetto. White institutions created it, white institutions maintain it and white society condones it. White racism is essentially responsible for the explosive mixture, which has accumulated in our cities since the end of World War II.[100]

All the programs in the world aimed at changing the victims of racism will ultimately be useless if those institutions and structures that create them and control the conditions in the first place are not changed. This is very hard to accept for those who are White because your own happiness and lifestyle depend on these institutions and structures in their present form.

No one has made Whites see that the condition of the minority of our citizens is a direct product of the majority's struggle for happiness. It is, therefore, not surprising that all your effort to solve the problems in African-Americans' communities have caused so much frustration and met with so little success. You have tried to limit the effects of the dross without cutting off its flow. You have tried to help others to change without realizing that it requires change in yourselves.

It is not that African-Americans do not need or want to change. Just the opposite is true. However, Whites assume the victims themselves cause their problems rather than the institutions of the victimizers. And Whites assume that the cure for African-Americans illnesses begins with African-Americans and needs to be administered by Whites. And then, to add the final blow, the very institutions that created the problem in the first place administer the "cure."

It is as though an airplane were spraying poison gas over a city, causing the inhabitants to sicken and die. The owners of the airplane neither admit to the poisoning nor promise to stop. They do, however, sign a contract to develop an antidote for the gas. While the antidote is being developed, the gassing continues. When the antidote is ready, the pilots are directed to spray it, together with the poison gas, when they next fly over the city. White society is deeply implicated in the ghetto. White institutions created it, White institutions maintain it, and White society condones it. White racism is essentially responsible for the explosive mixture.

If we were to double or triple our efforts to bring about change for the victims of racism through increased housing, better education, more employment, and other social improvements, we might achieve some statistical progress. However, we would set two opposing forces in the White society into even greater contradiction with each other: (1) the force that creates and perpetuates inhuman conditions, (2) and the force that tries to correct the results. Thus the sickness itself, which is not in the communities of African-Americans but in the White community, goes unchallenged because you are trying to change the wrong people. The name of this problem is *"White Racism."* The only way to deal with it is by changing the systems and institutions of the United States that dominate, control, and exploit African-Americans for the benefit of the Whites.

There is no soft, polite way to discuss this problem. The name by which it must be called is "White Racism." To call it anything else is to avoid the real issue, and there are few problems we try harder to avoid. No other less offensive designation is accurate. There is no way of approaching the subject indirectly. It is the unique problem of White America. It is White racism. Simply changing attitudes is not enough. Helping victims of racism is not enough. Only reducing the power that enforces prejudice will enable significant progress in dismantling White racism.

Whites, you not only hold the power of racism in your hands, you are unable to let it go. You are prisoners of your own racism. The power of racism, which hurts and destroys African-Americans, also hurts and destroys you as White-Americans. In a sophisticated process of incorporation, every White person in America is willingly or unwillingly made a permanent participant in America's system of White Racism. Individually and corporately, White-Americans are enslaved in racism and need to be set free. You never wanted to be racist. You still don't. For a long time you even thought you weren't, but now you know you are. And you know how you got this way. Whenever you think about it, it ought to enrage you and cause you to feel hurt deep inside yourselves. It is not guilt you feel—not anymore—just burning pain and anger over the fact that you were made into a racist. It happened to you. Whether you like it or not, you were made into a racist. And you are still one. It should make you angry.

If only it were as simple a problem as intentional racism! But our definition of racism, prejudice plus power, means that all of you who are White are part of and inseparable from a society that continually and systematically subordinates people of color. Whether or not you are intentional bigots, you are all locked inside a system of structural racism. As White-Americans, every White person supports, benefits from, and is unable to be separated from White Racism. As White oppressors, you are yourselves oppressed. The jailer is imprisoned and the victimizer victimized. You are prisoners in the racist structures of American society, and you need to be set free. The same fetters that bind the captive bind the captor, and the White-Americans are captive of their own myths, woven so clearly and so imperceptibly into the fabric of our national experience.[101]

In the White-American mentality, nothing could be more abrasive to you than the idea that you are not free. As White-Americans you sing, speak, and pray about yourselves as people who are already free, whose freedom is already attained and needs only to be preserved with diligence and shared with missionary zeal. You are the people who fought off colonial oppression and gained your independence. Your country is called "the land of the free and the home of the brave." You give thanks to God at least every Fourth of July and Thanksgiving Day that you are a free people and that you no longer have to struggle for your freedom like most other people in the world.

Whites' belief that you are already free has been the determining factor in setting the goals for resolving racial conflicts. You begin with the assumption that African-Americans need and want to become free like you. You want to help them "come up to your level." When you speak of equality, you mean you want them to become equal to you. All of these goals proclaim that you do not need to change or become free yourselves. You have difficulty believing that you, too, as well as African-Americans, are oppressed and need liberation.

The church with other institutions in contemporary society remains captive to the continued systemic racism of the present and is to a great extent still unrepentant for it. Most Whites are horrified by the distortions of Christianity taught by White supremacist organizations and other right wing fundamentalists. Their misuse of God's name to defend hatred and exploitation appalls you. But the responsibility for this misuse does not lie only with those who openly sow the seeds of racial hatred. To your great shame, your own mainline churches have all too often allowed themselves to be identified with racial supremacist thinking. And when the times called for forceful and courageous proclamation of the truth based on clear biblical understanding, your churches, and you yourselves, have often turned aside because of internal pressures and political expediency. This unfaithfulness has resulted in continued confusion about the content of Scripture and Christian teaching as well as the scandalous reality that the church today is still the most radically segregated institution in the United States.

So what's the answer? The answer is in the hands of White-Americans. The solution cannot come from African-Americans. Expecting an answer from them is like expecting the lion to look at the lamb and say, "What is the answer to your fear and frustration, little lamb?" We know what the problem is; it has been well outlined statistically and historically. The problem is White Racism.

Now what is the answer to the problems of African-Americans? The answer is in the will and power of White society and White institutions to change. Whites must change. In addressing the problem of African-Americans, White-Americans must first of all acknowledge the past. St. Thomas Aquinas said that God's omnipotence has only one limitation. "Even God," said Aquinas, "cannot make the past not to have been." Our past cannot be denied or forgotten. Our only hope is that it be forgiven.

Christians are answerable to a story that says that God forgives us, even from the cross. The divine willingness to take us back is not based upon some sort of cheap grace; a cross is not cheap. Christian forgiveness begins in God's amazing determination to have a family, in God's relentless pursuit of

210

us even into the wilderness.

One of the most extraordinary signs of God's grace is the willingness of African-American Christians to seek reconciliation with White Christians, to obey Jesus and to love their enemies, despite their enemies' lack of contrition. That any African-American remains Christian at all is a miracle, since their forefathers were told that Christianity justified slavery.

What could be more powerful than for White Christians to accept forgiveness by realizing that you need not deny past sins so that your stories, as Whites and as African-Americans, can be transformed into the common story of being Christian? Our quarrel with America's current cinema of denial is not that it is uniquely evil, though it is that, but rather that it is the wrong story.

Karl Barth said forgiveness precedes repentance. Only as forgiven people are we free to confess. Without a story of God's redemption, we are condemned ceaselessly to be trapped in the tiresome rituals of denial and falsification. With that story embraced as our own, we are free, we can breathe; and those whose differences and history made them our enemies can become even more than our friends. They can become family.

Conclusion: What Do We Do Now?

Perhaps, like us, you have found these words from Scripture and from history convicting. We have not been and are not now the reconciling people God calls us to be. But we want to be. We want to combat racism and injustice. Where do we begin?

The editors of this volume do not claim to have all the answers to that question. Injustice and racism are long-standing and deep-seated problems that we cannot easily solve. We too are stumbling as we search for concrete ways to be reconciled and to have reconciling attitudes. In offering some suggestions of first steps toward reconciliation, we hope others in our churches will discover specific actions that can promote justice and make us one in Christ.

PRAYER AND FASTING

Prayer is a recognition that it is Christ, not we ourselves, who reconciles us. The demons of injustice and racism will not be cast out except through prayer and fasting. Perhaps the greatest reason we have failed to live out the social implications of the gospel is that we have relied too much on our own power and solutions. Only the grace of God through Jesus our Lord can move our hearts to love. Only the wisdom of God through the Holy Spirit can give us solutions to the injustice of society. Only hope in the kingdom Jesus promised can motivate us to work for reconciliation.

INTEGRITY IN TELLING OUR STORY

As individuals and as corporate bodies of Christ, we must tell the truth about ourselves and our history. Continued false politeness—in the name of social or political correctness—cannot bring the confession and repentance necessary for healing. We cannot continue to absolve ourselves from history or hide from our family dysfunction. We also cannot continue allowing that past to control our present and future. We must openly and honestly confront the systemic circumstances that leave us a racially divided people.

PUBLIC REPENTANCE AND APOLOGIES

Another step toward forgiveness and reconciliation is repentance. This might include the leaders of our colleges and of our churches acknowledging past injustices. At first, this may strike us as unfair and counterproductive—How do we apologize for the mistakes of others? Were not our church and college leaders doing the best they could in a racist time?

Perhaps. Perhaps not. There is no doubt that in many cases those leaders were sinfully racist. More importantly, we must stop justifying the intended racism and the unintended consequences of our well-meaning spiritual ancestors.

But what good can such public apologies do? If we personally are not racist and if we are trying to make our schools and churches places of justice, then what good does it do to rake up the injustices of the past? Much good, actually. By repenting of the sins of our ancestors, we can begin to make specific restitution to the victims of that injustice. We also can admit our own positions of privilege have often come as a result of actions and attitudes we ourselves hate, but nevertheless happened to our benefit and others' detriment. It may be that the hurt and pain cannot be undone, only forgiven in the grace Jesus brings. But we should offer whatever specific fruits of repentance we can, for the sake of Jesus and for the love of our brothers and sisters.

PARTNERS FOR CHANGE

Recognizing the long history of separate (and not equal) White and African-American churches, efforts can be made on both sides to form cooperative efforts to bring economic and spiritual help to impoverished communities. Such efforts as CCSI in Nashville, a partnership between the Woodmont Hills church (White) and the Schrader Lane church (African-American), can provide the very help that Greene pleads for in restoring human dignity and economic independence. Rather than being one more patronizing effort on the part of the White church, such cooperation points us toward true equality. Such cooperation will require us to place the needs of people above perceived doctrinal differences, again pointing us to unity in Christ above all else.

INTEGRATED CHURCHES

For too long both African-Americans and Whites have excused our segregated churches by claiming "people are just more comfortable with their own kind." After all, segregated churches allow Christians to experience the type of preaching, singing, worship, and service they prefer.

Precisely. Which is the root of the problem. For our sake Jesus left the comfort of heaven. For our sake he refused his own preferences ("let this cup pass from me") to do the will of God. Christ does not call us to comfort but to neighbor love. He does not ask what we prefer, but calls us to the cross, where we put the preferences of our brothers and sisters before our own. If we are serious about justice and racial equality, then we must reach out in our neighborhoods. This means churches must refuse to relocate to the suburbs when their neighborhoods change. It means we must allow cultural differences in our churches. It means we should target other races in our evangelism. It means the integration of ministry staff and leadership teams, so that at the leadership level, our churches begin to model the message. It might mean some of us should consider becoming part of a congregation made up predominately of those of another race.

Personal Friendship

We will not eliminate injustice and racism solely through better interpersonal relations, but it is a healthy first step. The command of Jesus to love one's neighbor requires more than knowing the family next door (who more than likely are of our race and economic standing). This will require great intentionality. We must purposely seek circumstances that place us in contact with people of different ethnic and racial backgrounds. It means making friends with those of another race. By eating, working, and playing with those economically and socially different from us, we can begin to understand, appreciate, and genuinely love them. Such friendships would not only reduce personal prejudices but would help eliminate the "good-old-boy network" that perpetuates inequality in hiring and housing.

Particular Help to the Oppressed

When one mentions "social justice" in many Churches of Christ, one immediately faces objections. "Why should we worry about current injustice? If we work to make our current society better, isn't that like rearranging the deck chairs on the *Titanic*? Isn't the world lost? It's the gospel, not social programs, that people really need."

We hope this study on the biblical basis of social justice has answered those objections. In Churches of Christ we have so emphasized individual salvation and so feared a "social gospel" that we have generally neglected the radical implications of living in the kingdom of God. We often express our gratitude for the blessings of being Americans—freedom, democracy, and a free-market economy—but fail to see that these are in some aspects mixed blessings. Freedom is not fully experienced by victims of institutionalized racism. Democracy can mean the tyranny of the majority over the minority. A free market economy can harm those at the bottom of the economic ladder.

We in the church cannot assume that America will care for all those in need. We dare not blind ourselves to injustice. Instead, our churches must develop programs to serve the poorest of the poor. Our churches must be at the forefront of those who expose injustice and campaign for just policies. No Christian can in good conscience vote for a candidate on the basis of self-interest. The question is not whether we are better off than four years ago; the question is whether those in genuine need are better off.

Specific programs our congregations already sponsor include literacy classes, school supply programs, providing both temporary and permanent housing, counseling and adoption services, nursing care, and a host of others. We must be creative in the power of the Lord to allow his justice to roll down like a mighty stream. We must move beyond individual good will and friendship, and even beyond congregational programs to broader, societal justice.

Further Reading

Anderson, David and Brent Zuercher. *Letters Across the Divide: Two Friends Explore Racism, Friendship, and Faith.* Grand Rapids: Baker, 2001.

DeYoung, Curtiss Paul. *Coming Together: The Bible's Message in an Age of Diversity.* Valley Forge, PA: Judson Press, 1995.

Emerson, Michael O. and Christian Smith. *Divided by Faith: Evangelical Religion and the Problem of Racism in America.* New York: Oxford University Press, 2000.

Evans, Tony. *Let's Get to Know Each Other: What White and Black Christians Need to Know About Each Other.* Nashville: Thomas Nelson, 1995.

McKenzie, Steven L. *All God's Children: A Biblical Critique of Racism.* Louisville, KY: Westminster/John Knox, 1997.

Okholm, Dennis L., ed. *The Gospel in Black and White: Theological Resources for Racial Reconciliation.* Downers Grove, IL: InterVarsity Press, 1997.

Peart, Norman Antony. *Separate No More: Understanding and Developing Racial Reconciliation in Your Church.* Grand Rapids: Baker, 2000.

Perkins, Spencer and Chris Rice. *More than Equals: Racial Healing for the Sake of the Gospel.* Downers Grove, IL: InterVarsity Press, 1993.

Washington, Raleigh, Glen Kehrein, and Claude V. King. *Breaking Down the Walls: Experiencing Biblical Reconciliation and Unity in the Body of Christ.* Chicago: Moody Press, 1997.

Endnotes

1. On justice in the OT, see Abraham J. Heschel, *The Prophets, Vol. 1* (New York: Harper Colophon Books, 1969), p. 195-220, and Gerhard Von Rad, *Old Testament Theology, Vol. 1* (New York: Harper & Brothers, 1962), 370-382. Those preaching on the Minor Prophets will find the following material helpful: Elizabeth Achtemeier, *Minor Prophets I New International Biblical Commentary* (Peabody, MA: Hendrickson, 1996); Elizabeth Achtemeier, *Preaching from the Minor Prophets*, (Grand Rapids: Eerdmans, 1998); James Limburg, *Hosea-Micah Interpretation Commentary* (Atlanta: John Knox, 1988); Harold Shank, *Minor Prophets Vol. 1 Hosea-Micah* (Joplin, MO: College Press, 2001).

2. In the Hebrew, the root of righteousness is *ṣedeq*. Justice is *mišpāt*. Righteousness appears in Hosea 2:19; 10:12; 14:9. The root meaning justice occurs at 2:19; 5:1, 11; 6:5; 7:7; 10:4; 12:6; 13:10; 14:9.

3. Psalms 50:6; 89:14; 97:2; 103:10; Zephaniah 3:5. The word appears in Hosea at 2:19; 12:6.

4. Deuteronomy 32:4; Isaiah 28:17; 30:18.

5. The Hebrew word is *ḥesed* and appears in Hosea at 2:19; 4:1; 6:4, 6; 10:12; 12:6.

6. The King James Version uses twelve different English words to translate *ḥesed*.

7. The Hebrew is *raḥam* appearing in Hosea at 1:6, 7; 2:1, 4, 19, 23; 14:3.

8. The Hebrew word is *'āman* from which we get "Amen" used in Hosea 2:20; 11:12.

9. Cf. Ruth 4:16; Esther 2:7 ("brought up" in the NIV).

10. The Hebrew word is *yādā'* and appears in Hosea 2:8, 20; 4:1, 6; 5:3-4, 9; 6:3, 6; 7:9; 8:2, 4; 9:7; 11:3; 13:4-5; 14:9.

11. Roland de Vaux, *Ancient Israel Vol. II* (New York: McGraw-Hill, 1965), 72-74.

12. This translation is from Eugene Peterson, *The Message: Old Testament Prophets in Contemporary Language* (Colorado Springs: NavPress, 2000).

13. The text assumes that God can feel pain. Genesis 6 is the first evidence of God feeling pain. It grieves God to his heart that he had created man. Ezekiel 16, with the extended metaphor of God finding Israel as the baby girl in the ditch, raising her up, marrying her, and falling in love with her only to watch her become a prostitute, is the story of tremendous pain, of God feeling pain. In the story of the Prodigal Son in Luke 15, the father represents God, another story suggesting that God feels pain.

14. Jonathan Kozol, *Amazing Grace: The Lives of Children and the Conscience of a Nation* (New York: Crown Publishers, 1995), 3, 186-189.

15. Ronald J. Sider, *Rich Christians in an Age of Hunger* (Dallas: Word, 1990).

16. Harold Shank, "Nashville's Central Church of Christ: The First 20 Years," *Restoration Quarterly* 41 (1999): 11-26.

17. Amos accuses North Israel of twelve specific wrongs: they sell defenseless people into slavery without cause (2:6), deny certain people access to courts (2:7; 5:10), sexually abuse poor women (2:7), fail to return items taken in pledge (2:8), collect unjust taxes and fines (2:8), force the poor to give them products (5:11), take bribes (5:12), defraud the poor in business transactions (8:5), tamper with weights and measures (8:5), use poor people as slave labor (8:6), sell inferior merchandise (8:6), and there is a strong suspicion that people are charged unfair rents (3:15-4:1). Amos describes the oppressors in ten ways: they own winter and summer houses (3:15), the women live in leisure (4:1), the oppressors dwell in stone mansions (5:11), they lead complacent and secure lives (6:1), they

sleep on beds decorated with ivory (6:4), they have time to lounge rather than work (6:4), they eat choice cuts of meat (6:4), they are at ease to enjoy the arts (6:5), they have ample supply of alcoholic beverages (6:6), and they use fine lotions (6:6).

18. This section on the four words for poverty summarizes the work of Thomas John Finley, "An Evangelical Response to the Preaching of Amos," *JETS* 28 (1985): 413-415. See a slightly longer treatment in Shank, *Minor Prophets*, 200-204.

19. The Hebrew word is *ṣadîq* used in 2:6; 5:12.

20. Proverbs talks about how lazy hands can make one poor. Sleeping too much and not working leads to poverty. A drunkard or glutton may become destitute (Proverbs 10:14; 20:13; 23:21).

21. Cf. a fuller treatment in Harold Shank and Wayne Reed, "A Challenge to Suburban Churches," *Journal of Interdisciplinary Studies* 7 (1995), 119-134.

22. The Hebrew word *'ebyôn* appears in Amos 2:6; 4:1; 5:12; 8:4, 6.

23. The Hebrew word is *dal* used in Amos 2:7; 4:1; 5:1; 8:6.

24. The Hebrew word is *'ānāw* used in Amos 2:7; 8:4.

25. The Hebrew word is *šā'ap* appearing in Amos 2:7; 8:4.

26. The Hebrew word is *'āšaq* from Amos 4:1.

27. The Hebrew word is *sārar* of Amos 5:12.

28. The Hebrew word is *bāšas* of Amos 5:11.

29. The common Hebrew word is *nāṭâ*, used in Amos 2:7, 8; 5:12.

30. The Hebrew word is *rāṣas* used in Amos 4:1.

31. Rolland E. Wolfe, "The Book of Micah," *The Interpreter's Bible* (Nashville: Abingdon, 1980), p. 904.

32. Walter Brueggeman in *The Prophetic Imagination* (Minneapolis: Fortress Press, 1978) explains how the prophets use words to create a picture of an alternative world.

33. John McKenzie, *A Theology of the Old Testament* (Garden City, NY: Doubleday, 1974), 27.

34. John Mark Hicks, *1 & 2 Chronicles* (Joplin, MO: College Press, 2000), 15-26.

35. See Christopher Begg, "'Seeking Yahweh' and the Purpose of Chronicles," *Louvain Studies* 9 (Fall 1982): 128-41 and G.E. Schaefer,

"The Significance of Seeking God in the Purpose of the Chronicler" (Th.D., Southern Baptist Theological Seminary, 1972).

36. J. G. McConville, "1 Chronicles 28:9: Yahweh 'Seeks Out' Solomon," *Journal of Theological Studies* ns37 (1986): 105.

37. Ibid., 108.

38. J. G. McConville, "I & II Chronicles," DSB (Philadelphia: Westminster, 1984), 99-100.

39. Kelly, 49-62.

40. Sara Japhet, *The Ideology of the Book of Chronicles and Its Place in Biblical Thought*, rev. ed., trans. Anna Barber (New York: Peter Lang, 1997), 191-8.

41. John Mark Hicks, *Yet Will I Trust Him: Understanding God in a Suffering World* (Joplin, MO: College Press, 1999), 131-5.

42. Roddy L. Braun, "1 Chronicles," WBC (Waco, TX: Word, 1986), 278.

43. Leslie C. Allen, "1, 2 Chronicles," CC (Waco, TX: Word, 1987), 189.

44. Ehud Ben Zvi, "A Gateway to the Chronicler's Teaching: The Account of the Reign of Ahaz In 2 Chr 28,1-27," *Journal for the Study of the Old Testament* 7 (1993): 243.

45. F. Scott Spencer, "2 Chronicles 28:5-15 and the Parable of the Good Samaritan," *Westminster Theological Journal* 46 (1984): 317-49; the chart was adapted from Spencer's on pages 320-1.

46. Ibid., 347.

47. H. G. M. Williamson, "1 and 2 Chronicles," NCB (Grand Rapids: Eerdmans, 1982), 368.

48. M. Patrick Graham, "Setting the Heart to Seek God: Worship in 2 Chronicles 30:1-31:1," In *Worship and the Hebrew Bible: Essays In Honour of John T. Willis*, ed. M. Patrick Graham, Rick R. Marrs, and Steven L. McKenzie (JSOTSup 284; Sheffield: Sheffield Academic Press, 1999), 141.

49. Richard L. Pratt, *1 and 2 Chronicles: A Mentor Commentary* (Fearn, Ross-Shire: Mentor, 1998), 433: "[Hezekiah] was no pedantic legalist, insisting on precise and wooden application of the Law. Hezekiah's situation was unusual and this extraordinary situation required the application of precedents in Mosaic Law in creative ways. The fact that Hezekiah postponed only one month

demonstrates the king's desire to adhere to Mosaic standards, but his unique situation required ingenious application."

50. Terry L. Eves, "The Role of the Passover in the Book of Chronicles: A Study of 2 Chronicles 30 and 35" (Ph.D., Annenberg Research Institute, 1992), 213.

51. See John Mark Hicks, *1 & 2 Chronicles* (Joplin, MO: College Press, 2001), 145-9.

52. Wright, *Jesus and the Victory of God*, (Minneapolis: Fortress Press, 1996), 288f. A significant part of the following reading of the Beatitudes is indebted to Wright's account.

53. There have been, of course, all sorts of sociological studies bearing witness to the power of "civil religion" in the United States. Even though civil religion invokes the name "God," and prays to "God," and sings "God bless America," this does not mean this is the same god as that revealed in Jesus Christ. Jesus would have us probe, it appears, the agenda of those prayers and songs and invocations: Is the agenda a nationalistic triumph of "good" or "democracy" or "civilization"? Or the Kingdom of Heaven? Seldom, of course, are these two different agendas seen as mutually exclusive, making the matter more messy in practice. That is, in both Israel's day and ours, nationalistic triumph is seen as part and parcel of the triumph of God's rule.

54. See Psalm 2:8 where the "ends of the earth" are promised to the "Son of God" who will come bearing a "rod of iron." The promise of the "ends of the earth" here in Psalm 2 is precisely the temptation set before Jesus during his time of testing in the wilderness. In other words, the temptation stories themselves can be read (and have been read by numerous commentators) not as some generalized set of temptations experienced by universal humanity (such as lust of the flesh, lust of the eyes, and the pride of life), but instead as a set of Messianic options from which Jesus had to choose: would it be as a welfare king ("command that these stones be made bread"), as a religious reformer (the temptation to something of an epiphany in the temple courts), or as geo-political head of empire ("I'll give you all the nations of the earth")? For such an interpretation and references to other similar interpretations, see J.H. Yoder, *The Politics of Jesus*, 2nd. ed. (Grand Rapids: Eerdmans, 1994), 24ff.

55. Wright, 288f.

56. Ibid., 289.

57. Each of the following categories is discussed in a number of places. See Howard Thurman, *Jesus and the Disinherited* (Boston: Beacon Press, 1976), and John Howard Yoder, "The Original Revolution," in *For the Nations: Essays Public and Evangelical* (Grand Rapids: Eerdmans, 1976).

58. Reinhold Niebuhr, though, is an interesting specimen in this regard. While he takes Jesus to be advocating complete non-resistance in the Sermon on the Mount, Niebuhr claims as well that Jesus' teaching is not relevant to human history. That is, if you want to be relevant to the social and political world, then you will not seek to live out the teaching of Jesus, but instead will seek "justice." In this system then, Niebuhr could advocate, according to his "Christian realism," that the United States could not but pursue the nuclear arms race, as it helped maintain a balance of power.

59. Cited in Richard Gardner, "Matthew," *Believers Church Bible Commentary Series*, eds. Elmer A. Martens and Howard H. Charles (Scottdale, PA: Herald Press, 1991), 101.

60. Martin Luther King, "Letter from Birmingham Jail," in *A Testament of Hope: The Essential Writings and Speeches of Martin Luther King, Jr.*, ed. James M. Washington (San Francisco: Harper, 1991), 300.

61. Walter Wink, *Engaging the Powers: Discernment and Resistance in a World of Domination* (Minneapolis: Fortress, 1992), chapter nine.

62. Ibid., 176.

63. Ibid., 178.

64. Ibid.

65. Some interpret Jesus as standing in stark contrast to the Old ("you have heard it said . . . *but I say . . .*"). But an interpretation of Jesus' teachings here as requiring non-violence does not depend upon such a viewpoint; i.e., if the original cultural intention of the *lex talionis*, as many commentators suggest, was to *limit* retaliation, then Jesus accepts that intention and simply deepens it here.

66. There is also a question about the translation of the dative expression *to ponero*. This is typically taken as substantive (i.e., do not resist *evil*, do not resist *an evil doer*, etc.). If *to ponero*, instead,

is taken as an instrumental dative, we get another sense: "do not resist by evil means." See Glen Stassen, "The Fourteen Triads of the Sermon on the Mount," presented at Society of Christian Ethics, 2001. http://www.fuller.edu/sot/faculty/stassen/14Triads.htm.

67. Foy E. Wallace, *The Sermon on the Mount and the Civil State* (Nashville: Foy E. Wallace Jr. Publications, 1967), ix. Emphasis *his*. Cf. repetition of the kingdom is a "reign of heaven in the hearts of men" on 65.

68. Ibid., 21, 24, 33.

69. Ibid., 106.

70. Parts of this chapter is reprinted from Douglas A. Foster, "An Angry Peace: Race and Religion," *ACU Today* (Spring 2000):8-20, 39 with permission from *ACU Today* and Abilene Christian University.

71. Hebert Gutman, *The Black Family in Slavery and Freedom* (New York: Pantheon Books, 1976).

72. Dinesh D'Souza, *The End of Racism* (New York: The Free Press, 1995), 97.

73. Paul Craig Roberts, "Declining Power of Truth" *Investor's Business Daily* (March 15, 1999).

74. Bernice Dorssett, "From Streets of Gold" (unpublished book-length manuscript).

75. "Brown, Racial Change, and the Civil Rights Movement," *Virginia Law Review* 80:7 (1994): see also Jackson Draft Opinion, *Brown v. Board of Education* (March 15, 1954), Library of Congress, Jackson Papers, Box 184, case file: segregation cases, on file with the Virginia Law Review Association, 66.

76. As quoted in Larry Elder, *The Ten Things You Can't Say In America* (St. Martin's Griffin, New York, 2000), 12.

77. In George Reisman, "Capitalism: The Cure for Racism," *C-SPAN* (October 23, 1996).

78. Booker T. Washington, *Up from Slavery* (New York: Doubleday, Page and Company, 1901), 149.

79. William Raspberry, "The Myth That Is Crippling Black America," *Reader's Digest* (August 1990): 96-98.

80. Dale Mezzacappa, "Dreams Deferred," *Philadelphia Inquirer* (April 25, 1999).

81. Sidney M. Wilhelm, *Who Needs The Negro?* (Garden City, NY: Anchor Books, 1971), 332-334.

82. Unwed fathers are much less likely to pay child support than separated or divorced fathers. In 1983, for example, fewer than 18 percent of unwed mothers over age 18 were awarded child support, and only 14 percent reported that they received any. The percentage was smaller for others receiving aid for families with dependent children. Willie Wofford, "A Father's Duty," *Ebony*, (June, 1988): 10.

83. U.S. Bureau of the Census, "Current Population Reports: Money, Income and Poverty Status of Families and Persons in the United States," 1999.

84. "Black Americans' Perceptions of the Socio-Historical Role of the Church," Robert Joseph Taylor, Michael Thornton, and Linda Chatters, *Journal of Black Studies*, Vol. 18 No. 2, (December 1987): 123-138.

85. Ibid.

86. Ibid.

87. Ibid.

88. Ibid.

89. Carol Rust, "Man of Principle, Pastor Kirbyjon Caldwell," *Continental*, (October 2001): 42.

90. "Church Businesses Spread the Gospel of Self-Help," *Ebony* (February 1987): 61-68.

91. *The United Methodist Hymnal*, no. 353.

92. Benjamin Demott, *The Trouble with Friendship: Why Americans Can't Think Straight about Race* (New York: Atlantic Monthly, 1995).

93. Ibid., pp.30-31.

94. Ibid.

95. Quoted in Benjamin DeMott, *"Put on a Happy Face,"* in *Harper's Magazine* 291 (September 1995): 34.

96. As quoted in DeMott, *The Trouble with Friendship*, 37.

97. John Hope Franklin, *The Color Line Legacy for the Twenty-first Century* (Columbia: University of Missouri Press, 1993), 74.

98. U.S. Commission on Civil Rights, *Racism in America and How to Combat It* (Washington, 1970).

99. National Education Association, *Education and Racism* (Washington, 1973).

100. See the *Report of the National Advisory Commission on Civil*

Disorders, known as the Kerner Report (New York: Bantam Books, 1968).

101. C. Eric Lincoln, *Race, Religion and the Continuing American Dilemma* (New York: Hill and Wang, 1984), 3.

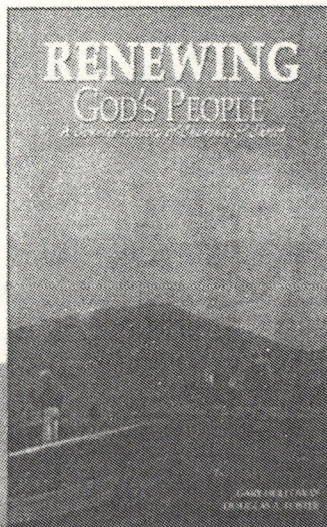

What's Right With the Church?

ISBN 0-89112-020-3 $15.95

- What are the good things about our heritage?
- Why haven't we engaged more vigorously with the societal issues of our day?
- What does it mean to place our hope in the kingdom of God?

In this important book, Richard Hughes suggests answers to these and other vital questions for Christians of the American Restoration Heritage.

Hughes cuts to the chase, asking the critical questions: What were the strengths of the restoration vision? Is the vision still valid? Is scripture to be read as a blue-print (emphasizing rules) or as a narrative (emphasizing overarching principles)?
Mike Cope - Minister
Highland Church of Christ, Abilene Tx

No one has thought more about the history and future of Churches of Christ than Richard Hughes. In this volulme he powerfully domonstrates how an understanding of our history can help us be more biblical, more faithful to the cross, and more devoted to the cause of God.
Doug Foster
Professor of Church History and Director of the Center for Restoration Studies
Abilene Christian University

In these essays, Richard Hughes issues a heart felt call to reclaim a vision kof the Kingdom of God... if Churches of Christ are to survive, they need to hear t his radical plea for a counter-cultural ethical vision.
Gary Holloway
Professor of Bible
Lipscomb University

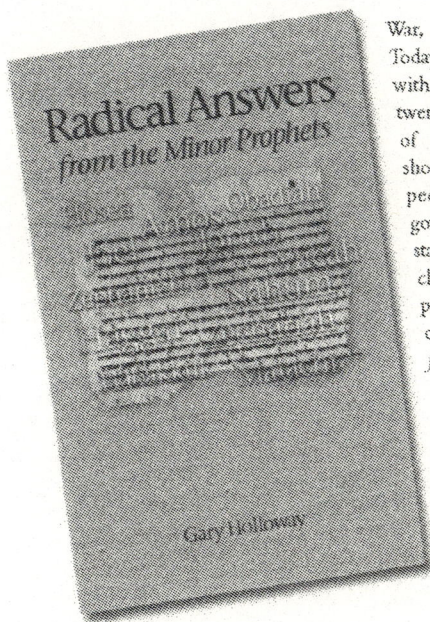